THE STOIC'S GUIDE TO A PEACEFUL LIFE

A MODERN APPROACH TO EMBRACING STOICISM FOR MENTAL RESILIENCE, EMOTIONAL CONTROL, AND PERSONAL CHANGE, EVEN IF YOU'RE A BEGINNER

JORDAN T. BECKETT

For Justin

INTRODUCTION

There has never been a greater need for strong, resilient thinkers than right here, right now. And I don't mean the lucky few who step out of the cradle, fully capable of taking on anything life throws at them. I mean a whole generation of sturdy, empathetic creatives who have clocked the hours and worked through the pain necessary to grow into the people they are destined to become. The people we all need them to be. I want to tell you about one such person now.

Mark couldn't seem to get anything right. A black cloud of unlucky coincidences seemed to follow him wherever he went. It's not that he wasn't smart; he just couldn't catch a break.

I met Mark when he was a freshman in college. By the end of his senior year, he'd had two deaths in his family, broken three ribs in a ski accident, and lost his academic scholarship.

None of us would have faulted Mark if he had chosen to have a seismic breakdown due to all the stress he was experiencing. Each trauma-inducing catastrophe was slowly chipping away at the healthy, whole person he was before, right? Unfortunately, the human condition is one of constant fracturing. For the most part, we are born happy and whole, but as we progress through life, tragedy rears its ugly head and beckons us to respond with cynicism and apathy.

However, Mark did not have a breakdown of seismic proportions. Mark began college a scared and uncharismatic wallflower. By his senior year, he was the strongest and wisest person I knew. Everyone went to him for advice, and his advice was always spot on. He never pulled his punches, but he never said anything untrue.

Eventually, I grew too curious to leave it alone. I asked one day how he had become the man he was despite all his challenges. Life had given him ample opportunities to make up an excuse, throw his arms into the air, and give up. And yet he had done the opposite; he was leaning into life now more than ever. What gives?

"Your strength lies within your mind," he said. "Not

in your ability to change what's outside of it." He then handed me a copy of a book that planted the seeds that would inspire me to write the book you are now holding. It was Meditations by Marcus Aurelius, the classic second-century Stoic text from the Roman philosopher king's journal entries.

You may be reading this and thinking, "I'd rather undergo a root canal than read second-century Stoic literature, so back off, Jordan." Hey, I get it. That being said, I was hoping you could stick with me a little longer before you chuck this book across the room. I promise you won't regret it.

If you're reading this book, you probably know at least a little bit about Stoicism. Maybe all you know is that it's a type of philosophy. Perhaps you know that it was first created in Ancient Greece before becoming popular in the Roman Empire. Maybe you've heard of some of its more famous thinkers like Epictetus and Seneca.

In case you know nothing, Stoicism is a philosophy of life created in the 3rd century BCE that has survived to the modern day. Stoicism is a philosophy of life because instead of thinking about abstract ideas (primarily the basis of other philosophical ideologies), Stoic philosophers thought deeply about problems genuinely connected to our lived experiences. Stoicism isn't attempting to identify the meaning of life, nor does it attempt to navigate metaphysical theories; it's trying to determine how we can savor and experience our lives rather than just live them.

Stoicism addresses questions like: *What does it mean to live a good life? How should we approach adversity? What does it mean to have virtue? What is the role of the individual in society?*

If you're reading this book, you've probably asked yourself some version of these questions before. Which is good! It means you care. The moment we collectively stop asking ourselves such questions is when society begins to falter.

It is precisely people like you who provide hope for the future. You are thoughtful and curious and have the best intentions at heart. Many people desire to be a force for good, but the road to goodness is paved with sense and self-awareness.

The only problem? The seeming lack of societal intention and individual self-awareness is currently circulating through our communities. Everywhere you turn, people seek to turn a profit. We point fingers instead of using our hands to build others up.

Let me be clear; the score is not: us good/them bad. Not at all. These are confusing times, with many highly vocal groups giving contradictory messaging. Many answer the call of hedonism, which admonishes us to pursue pleasure above all else. Can there be too much of a good thing? Others prefer to "rise and grind" and operate under the understanding that you have to pave your way in this world.

Today, mentors genuinely interested in their mentee's success are scarce. Many people are telling us what to think, what to eat, how to live, and how to work. In the age of "influencers," more people than ever before now receive large platforms with eager audiences. Those we follow and model ourselves after must be carefully vetted.

The fact of the matter is we're all new to this thing called life. We all are searching for inspiration and motivation to keep going. We are all looking for leadership from those who have gone before us, to offer up insight. If this sounds familiar, you may be parched for a glass of refreshing, compassionate wisdom. Well, thirst no more, my friend. Even if today's influencers are uninterested or unable to give you the soul food you need, the influencers of yesterday are.

Now, you may be thinking to yourself, "Jordan, I don't like old people that much. Let alone people who were born two thousand years ago. Why should I read some dusty, dumb journal entries from a guy who knows nothing about me?"

That's where I come in. I understand where you're coming from; I do. It took me a long time to work my way through these dusty old books. The language is outdated. The pacing is slow. The points they want to make can often be vague and indirect. But in all honesty, it was worth it to me. The diamonds in the rough shone through on every page, and I couldn't help but dig my way through. And now I want to pass it on to you.

I will give you the teaser trailer for one of the world's most successful philosophies. This book is a crash course into a worldview that is explicitly anti-fragile. It will provide you with down-to-earth, practical advice on applying Stoic ideas and principles to your daily life. That includes strategies for managing stress and anxiety, cultivating positive relationships, and finding purpose in everyday existence.

I will help you develop your Stoic practice by providing exercises and activities that bring the concepts to life. Ultimately, this book will serve as a valuable resource for anyone seeking to live with a greater sense of fulfillment and meaning in a world that can often feel chaotic and overwhelming. But there's a catch. You have to put in the effort to bring the ideas to fruition. It's not enough to be able to recite quotes; you have to live them to receive the benefit.

This will be the first exercise in changing your

worldview for many of you. Congratulations, there's nothing to be scared of. It is the purest expression of freedom to be able to change your mind. You are doing the work of your highest self when you question your perceptions and seek to understand the world as best as possible.

It'll be like shaking the dust off your eyes and seeing the sunshine for the first time, like rising from a long nap and realizing that the heavy weight of sleep no longer sits on your shoulders. It's a beautiful thing, a happy thing, to see the world from a place of strength. And I'm going to help get you there.

ONE
IT'S A HARD-KNOCK LIFE

"You have power over your mind—not outside events. Realize this, and you will find strength."

MARCUS AURELIUS

Before we get all Love and Light, let's dive deeper into why Stoicism is necessary in the modern world. To be clear, the reason isn't because things are going super. Things are rough out there. We're not the first generation to say it, and we won't be the last. Still, it feels like the fabric holding society together is sometimes fraying at the seams.

The problem with describing the often overwhelming number of societal ills that plague us today is that it comes across as whiney and overly dramatic to anyone who doesn't already see them. To these people, it seems you're conjuring problems out of thin air when there's no reason to do so. This can cause a significant rift between people trying to understand each other.

Someone from an older generation may have a different sense of what type of world the younger generations are experiencing. Older generations are no longer trying to start a career or a family in the present day; there isn't the same level of interaction with the world as younger generations trying to carve out a place for themselves.

The media doesn't really help, either. Suppose your primary source of information is saying one thing, and someone else's source is saying another. In that case, it can be hard to reconcile the two. Despite these difficulties, we're going to sit down and take a look at the world we live in. Grab a seat.

It may seem odd to start a book about Stoicism by describing all the world's problems. After all, one of the core tenets of Stoicism is the conscious acceptance of any and all things that happen to you. Especially the things that are out of your control. It's a radical acceptance of life in all of its muddy glory.

So I want you to remember that just because I am describing social ills doesn't mean I am suggesting we spend the next several hours applying black nail polish and listening to My Chemical Romance until we enter a dissociative state. Acknowledging these issues without letting them dominate our emotional well-being is possible.

Troubled Times

In some ways, the problems young adults face today are just new versions of age-old difficulties. In other ways, the issues they face are unprecedented. Their parents and grandparents also struggled to discover who they were as people, what they wanted to do for a career, and the social pressures of these endeavors.

The standard nomenclature for this predicament is an identity crisis. This crisis is compounded by the fact that younger generations' sense of community is evolving (and, in some cases, going extinct). The challenge of discovering who we are was often once mitigated by the feeling that there was a group to which we belonged. But for most people today, that feeling is gone.

Levels of social trust are at an all-time low.

According to the Edelman Trust Barometer, the United States is one of the most polarized countries in the entire world. US citizens cite a lack of shared identity as one of the biggest drivers of this polarization (alongside a general distrust in government). In fact, in 15 out of the 26 countries they surveyed, the majority of people felt that their country was "more divided today than in the past." In all but two countries, Saudi Arabia and the United Arab Emirates, at least one-third of the population felt this way.

So we live in a world where people increasingly feel alienated from the people they live with and the organizations that govern them. At a time when connection is a scarcity, coming of age can feel like an unfortunate voyage into a dark field of bloodied thorns.

Maybe, on some level, it's always been this way. Each generation feels as if their lived experience is worse than their predecessors. Perhaps we are just looking at the challenges of our time and blowing them out of proportion. It's hard to deny that we live in an age that does not favor the human need for connection, belonging, and camaraderie.

Society's disconnection and distrust are exacerbating other issues, as well. Take violence, for example. According to The Marshall Project, a nonpartisan news project focused on the criminal justice system, the public perception of violent crime rates is at odds with reality. The rate of violent crime has been decreasing since its peak in 1992. We are lucky enough to experience roughly half the amount of violent crime as we did thirty years ago. But at the same time, our perception is that crime is getting worse, with nearly 80% of Americans believing that violent crime is rising.

In a survey published by The Guardian, 70% of the 2,000 Gen Zs surveyed said they were worried about terrorist attacks even though terrorist attacks are incredibly rare. In reality, you are 9,000 times likelier to die in a car accident than you are from a terrorist attack. These fears are compounded by commentary on social media, the 24-hour news cycle, and the fire hydrant of information from which we are all drinking. It's no coincidence that half of Gen Z attribute their anxiety to social media use. It's like a stressful hall of mirrors we're all walking down, getting distorted representations of reality and feeling mildly queasy as we search for the exit.

These feelings of anxiety are compounded by our generation's money troubles. Did you know that home prices have increased over 110% in the past sixty years, while wages have only risen a meager 15%? Gen Z often spends more money than they have to keep up appearances. They are also more likely to lie about their financial situation and are less likely to put money into savings.

After the 2008 financial crisis, millennials entering the workforce found themselves competing for a shrinking number of open positions for well-paying jobs. Only a decade later, the Coronavirus arrived, and Millenials and Gen Z are struggling to eke out a living.

Financial uncertainty abounds. But who cares? It's just money, right? Well, maybe so, but the price of everyday goods is rising at unprecedented rates.

Furthermore, Artificial Intelligence has entered the chat, sweeping into the arena like a deluge, threatening to wash away anyone and everyone not tied down with ten-inch bolts. It can write faster, draw faster, flip burgers, and sell hot dogs for pennies on the dollar.

The automation of nearly every professional society sector is already here, even if it hasn't grown to its mature size. Today, you can still tell when a robot is writing your term paper. It's obvious when a robot picks up the phone or checks you out at the grocery store.

How we work will look drastically different in 10 to 15 years. As technology progresses, the need for human interference in supply chains, healthcare, and other fields diminishes. But pretty soon, there won't be any human truck drivers. No warehouse workers or delivery jobs. Society will have to restructure how we use humans in the workforce.

Maybe you're thinking, well, hey, that sounds pretty good. I don't really even like working. Well, neither do I, but the whole distribution of goods system is sitting precariously on this fundamental human activity: work. Only a handful of people are trying to make this transition smoother. The uncertain future looms, and everyone here on the ground feels it, consciously or unconsciously. These are confusing times. Every time we regain our balance, the rug is pulled out from under us again.

So here we are, looking for peace of mind, a sense of accomplishment, and a purpose. Where are we to turn to? Let's take a trip back to another era when things were chaotic and full of darkness and uncertainty. Maybe there we can find some answers.

Stress Test

Before we jump in, let's do a quick exercise. Everybody is different. We live different lives, have different strengths and weaknesses, and grow up under different circumstances.

We're going to start by assessing the situation. Here is a quick twenty-question quiz that you can use to evaluate your current state of mind. It is used to decipher which aspects of yourself you need to reconnect with the most because, despite the modern use of the word stoic to describe someone who is stone-faced and emotionless, Stoicism is a fantastic tool for emotional intelligence.

Think of the past two weeks and ask yourself how much each question seems relevant. Grab a sheet of paper and write down the number you pick for the answer: 1, 2, 3, or 4. I'll tell you what to do with it at the end.

IN THE PAST TWO WEEKS:

Events in my life that I had no control over made me irritable or frustrated.

1. Not at all
2. Sometimes
3. Often
4. All the time!

I felt inadequate.

1. Not at all
2. Sometimes
3. Often
4. All the time!

I felt overwhelmed by my responsibilities.

1. Not at all
2. Sometimes
3. Often
4. All the time!

My arms, hands, and legs were clenched even when I wasn't doing anything physical.

1. Not at all
2. Sometimes
3. Often
4. All the time!

I overreacted to small things that shouldn't have upset me.

1. Not at all
2. Sometimes
3. Often
4. All the time!

I snapped at the people around me for no good reason.

1. Not at all
2. Sometimes
3. Often
4. All the time!

I felt anxious, like something terrible was about to happen even when things were normal.

1. Not at all
2. Sometimes
3. Often
4. All the time!

My workload was becoming more than I could handle.

1. Not at all
2. Sometimes
3. Often
4. All the time!

I felt like my life was going off the rails.

1. Not at all
2. Sometimes
3. Often
4. All the time!

I worried that things would only get worse for me in the future.

1. Not at all
2. Sometimes
3. Often
4. All the time!

I felt powerless to change my circumstances for the better.

1. Not at all
2. Sometimes
3. Often
4. All the time!

My mouth felt dry.

1. Not at all
2. Sometimes
3. Often
4. All the time!

I felt impatient with the people around me or with situations I encountered.

1. Not at all
2. Sometimes
3. Often
4. All the time!

I felt like I was rushing around trying to get everything done, with not enough time in the day to accomplish it all.

1. Not at all
2. Sometimes
3. Often
4. All the time!

My thoughts were racing a mile a minute, more than was comfortable.

1. Not at all
2. Sometimes
3. Often
4. All the time!

I felt like I was going to have a panic attack.

1. Not at all
2. Sometimes
3. Often
4. All the time!

The things in my life that I used to enjoy seemed uninteresting.

1. Not at all
2. Sometimes
3. Often
4. All the time!

I found it difficult to sleep.

1. Not at all
2. Sometimes
3. Often
4. All the time!

I found it difficult to relax.

1. Not at all
2. Sometimes
3. Often
4. All the time!

I felt nervous even if I wasn't interacting with anyone.

1. Not at all
2. Sometimes
3. Often
4. All the time!

Now add up all of your answers.

- 1-20 | Living a mostly stress-free lifestyle.
- 20-60 | Moderate amounts of stress are likely.
- 60-80 | Stress is high and causing real problems.

THIS ISN'T MEANT to diagnose you clinically. It's for you to get a good sense of your internal position. You should check in with yourself occasionally and ask these types of questions. It's good mental hygiene to check in and give yourself a once-over to ensure things are working correctly.

Journal Prompts

Reflection on Society's State

In the chapter, there are references to feelings of societal breakdown, distrust, and polarization. Reflect on your own perceptions of society today. Do you agree with the idea that society is fraying at its seams? Why or why not? Consider your online and offline experiences and interactions and how they shape your views on societal cohesion and unity.

Navigating Information Overload and Media Perception

The chapter discusses potential distortions in our perceptions due to the influence of media. Reflect on a recent news event or social issue you've come across. How did your primary sources of information present it? In light of the information presented in this chapter, do you believe there's a gap between media representation and reality in certain areas? How do you ensure you're getting an accurate view of events or issues?

Economic Uncertainties and Work Landscape

Economic changes and technological advances like AI pose challenges and opportunities for everyone. The chapter touches on the financial uncertainties younger generations face and the imminent changes in the workforce. How do you feel about the current and future state of the job market, especially in the context of automation? Reflect on whether you believe society and education systems adequately prepare people for these changes. What skills or mindsets do you think will be crucial in the next decade?

Personal Stress and Stoicism

Using the 'Stress Test' presented in the chapter as a guide, delve deeper into your own sources of stress. Identify the three primary stressors in your life and reflect on why they might significantly impact you. Stoicism emphasizes the acceptance of circumstances beyond our control. Which of these stressors can you not change?

TWO
STOICISM: A TIMELESS MINDHACK

"No thing great is created suddenly, any more than a bunch of grapes or a fig. If you tell me that you desire a fig, I answer you that there must be time. Let it first blossom, then bear fruit, then ripen."

EPICTETUS

In times of chaos, great thinkers often look to the past for guidance. That's likely why you're here right now, reading this book. People have been around for a long time, and there has to have been someone somewhere at some point who had a decent grasp on reality.

Stoicism grew out of the muddy mess that was the beginning of the Common Era. Starting around 300 BCE, the people living around the Mediterranean Sea struggled with plagues, endless war, and enslavement. The Stoics used this hardship as fuel for their philosophy of life. I'm sure many people threw their hands up, called it the will of the gods, and kept their heads down. However, the great thinkers of the era were putting together a system of thought that could carry anyone through life's most significant challenges.

Zeno, the founder of Stoicism, was a wealthy Phoenician merchant who traded a costly dye. His life was changed forever when he was sailing across the sea, only to have his ship crash off the coast of Greece, costing him his entire fortune. He was destitute and stranded. While in a bookstore in Greece, he picked up a book by Socrates and thus was introduced to philosophy. From the ashes of his enormous (former) wealth, Stoicism was born.

His successor, the boxer Cleanthes, arrived in Athens with four dollars in his pocket. He could study philosophy during the day by working nights as a water collector. He was rewarded for his dedication by becoming the head of the Stoic School for 32 years.

Seneca was also born into wealth. The son of a statesman, he was at one point one of the wealthiest men in the country. But like Zeno before him, it was all taken away, this time at the hands of the emperor who exiled him for adultery. He spent eight years in isolation before being brought back by the mother of the next emperor, Nero. Seneca was Nero's tutor and lived in his court as an advisor. That may sound great, living in the lap of luxury once more. Still, Nero was one of the most cruel emperors in Roman history, known for his authoritarian penchant for bloodlust.

Marcus Aurelius, known as the last great emperor of Rome, had to contend with invading barbarians from the north and a five-year war with the Parthians. He was seemingly always at the battlefront and would later die of a plague that killed five million people, a whopping 5% of the population. For reference, if 5% of the population were to die today, that would be 400 million people, more than the entire U.S. population!

When the Stoics talked about accepting the parts of life outside our control, they talked about exile, poverty, and constant bloody war. They were speaking from experience. The mentality that the Stoics developed to cope with the stress was one of acceptance, emotional resilience, and goodwill towards those around you. You can think of them as mental habits that aim to make you healthier and happier. It's the ultimate life hack!

What Is Stoicism?

Let's take a step back. By now, you probably know why Stoicism is popular, what it can offer, and why it's necessary. But hold on, hold on. What are we even talking about? I mean, what even is Stoicism? Stoicism is a philosophy of life that aims to train the practitioner to endure any hardship while maintaining a positive state of mind. Let's break that down.

A philosophy of life is a genre of philosophy distinct from other genres as it focuses on the nature and purpose of human life. This type of philosopher might ask the question, 'What does it mean to live a good life?' This would differ from a more abstract philosopher asking, 'What is truth?' or 'What is the true relationship between body and mind?'

The difference between the genres is that a philosopher of life seeks answers that they can tangibly use in everyday life. If I have a firm conviction about what it means to live a good life, I can behave in a way that aligns with my beliefs. If I am strongly convinced about what truth is, I might struggle to manifest that belief in my daily life.

So Stoicism is a philosophy of life because the pursuit of the Stoic is to realize certain truths about the world they can then use in their actual human lives. Put another way, Stoicism pursues actionable truths about how to live as a human being. Although the answer may not surprise you, according to the Stoics, the best way to spend your life is likely not to binge-watch Netflix all the time and eat nothing but cheeseburgers. (Trust me, I've been there.) The Stoic mind is characterized by a willingness to stand face-to-face with reality, ready for any difficulty.

If the Stoics had a mascot, it would be an old-growth pine tree standing on a cliff overlooking the sea. Searing salt winds, lashing across the thick evergreen needles adorning its many strong branches. Stoicism's truths are so effective at helping people live better lives that they became the foundation for one of the modern world's most influential psychological treatments, Cognitive Behavioral Therapy (CBT). Aaron Beck, the father of CBT, wrote in his bestselling book, *Cognitive Therapy of Depression*, "The philosophical origins of cognitive therapy can be traced back to the Stoic philosophers."

CBT is widely used to treat depression, anxiety, substance abuse, and trauma, among many other psychological difficulties, and its benefits have been statistically proven to be more effective than medication or talk therapy across the board. Both Stoicism and CBT deal with perception. Specifically, the ability to see things simply and straightforwardly, as they are, without assigning a value judgment, like 'this is good' or 'that is bad.' The Stoics teach us that the suffering we experience because of misfortune is not inherent within the occurrence itself. Put another way, when bad things happen, we suffer because of our reaction to the event, not the event itself.

Take Zeno's shipwreck, for example. Here is a wealthy merchant, heir to generational prosperity. He's a hard worker; he travels with his own ship as it makes its way to foreign lands. A lot is riding on this sale. The dye he produces takes months of preparation and back-breaking labor. And then it sinks. Put yourself in his shoes. How would you react? Would you become angry? Despondent? In one cruel twist of fate, your merchant empire tumbles to the bottom of the sea, never to return. You are stranded on the shores of a foreign land without your friends and any money.

Zeno would go on to create one of the world's most significant philosophies, treasured by millions of people across centuries. He didn't know it then, but his shipwreck was a catalyst for the birth of Stoicism. "I made a prosperous voyage," Zeno would later joke. "When I suffered a shipwreck."

Let's play with this idea a little. Think of something really unfortunate, something that would be difficult to spin as a positive experience, like losing a job. If you apply Zeno's idea, a Stoic wouldn't necessarily celebrate the loss of their job. Still, they would accept the challenge life had chosen for them. They would use the experience as a catalyst for becoming a better version of themselves.

Now you might stop here and say, what's the point? Why would I want to shut off my emotions and plaster a smile across my face when something genuinely bad just happened to me? My dog just died, and you want me to stuff it down, saying my sadness is unnecessary? Back off; I loved my dog!

It's not really like that, though. Everything is better in moderation; even the most positive emotions can become unhealthy if taken to excess. If someone uses Stoic ideas to shut themselves off from their life, they aren't living the Stoic way. Stoicism is meant to engage you with reality, not help you escape it. Suppose you are trying to incorporate this life-affirming philosophy into your worldview. In that case, you shouldn't be waging war on your feelings from your castle on logic island.

The goal is to help both your emotional and rational selves coexist peacefully.

Stoicism does indeed tend to favor the rational side more; it is a philosophy, after all. Still, it contains insight into keeping your rational self from becoming too strong and drying out your personality in favor of cold, hard logic. It doesn't have to be one or the other; it can be both.

This balancing act can be broken down into what are known as the three disciplines: the discipline of desire, the discipline of action, and the discipline of assent.

The Discipline of Desire

Think of the discipline of desire as acceptance. In Latin, the phrase is amor fati or 'love of one's fate.' In Seneca's famous book The Enchiridion, he says, "Seek not for events to happen as you wish but wish events to happen as they do and your life will go smoothly and serenely." The more we push for our life to be something other than what it is, the more we become dissatisfied. We may feel that something out there will give us happiness. If only we had more money, a better romantic partner, or a bigger tv, we would stop fussing about it. We could finally relax, knowing that the missing thing had arrived and we are complete.

In reality, it never actually works that way. We work really hard to get a raise or a better-paying job, buy a house or a car, and then need even more money. We buy the latest tv in the biggest size, and two years later, it's considered out of style, no longer at the cutting edge. You guessed it, time for a new tv!

The more we accept the way our life is, the happier we become. We don't need to stress about how things could be different when they aren't. We can and should have goals and aspirations, but we can pursue them like we pursue the end of a nice long hike. We don't need to stress out about getting to the destination.

"Almost nothing material is needed for a happy life," Marcus Aurelius wrote. "For he who has understood existence." Our happiness comes from our perception of the world, not from the stuff we get in it.

The discipline of desire is about taming the excesses of our emotions. By living in a mindset of acceptance, we are decreasing the risk of anger, frustration, envy, and the like. We can engage with our life directly without filtering it through a lens of dissatisfaction.

The Discipline of Action

Next comes the discipline of action. This is the part of Stoicism that deals with the goal of life and how to achieve that goal. According to the Stoics, life's goal is eudaimonia, often translated as fulfillment or happiness.

So the goal of life is to be happy, not exactly a revolutionary idea, but a good idea nonetheless. The goal is not fame or wealth or power; it's living in such a way that you are at peace with your place in the world.

Almost everyone wants to be happy, so we're all on the same page already, but how do we get there? The Stoics describe the discipline of action as a set of virtues. Virtue is the only real good in this philosophy. Everything else is neutral or evil.

There are four Stoic virtues: wisdom, courage, justice, and temperance. We will explore the four virtues in greater detail in the next chapter. They are fundamental to the Stoic life and deserve their own space.

Virtue helps us live in harmony with the rest of humanity and the world, the key to the discipline of action. This discipline is sometimes referred to as Stoic philanthropy, meaning the love of humankind. We are told to love our fellow human beings to the same degree as we love ourselves.

The discipline dealing with the love of humanity is called the discipline of action because we are meant to act at all times for the good of everyone. Suppose we want others to achieve the goal of happiness. In that case, we must act accordingly, not just think pleasant thoughts in their general direction.

If the discipline of desire aims to temper our passions, the discipline of action aims to lovingly engage us with our communities. In his introduction of the three disciplines, Epictetus said of the discipline of action: "… I ought not to be unfeeling like a statue, but should maintain my relations, both natural and acquired, as a religious man, as a son, a brother, a father, a citizen."

If we aim at the good life, our community will play an important role. Humans are social creatures. You could be the most emotionally resilient person in the world, but if you don't care about the people around you, can you really be said to be happy? Antisocial behavior isn't something we usually associate with peace of mind or a sense of fulfillment, and for good reason.

There is a contradiction between the first two disciplines. The discipline of desire says we should accept what fate has given us. The discipline of action says we should work toward the betterment of humankind. So which is it, acceptance of fate or pursuit of something better?

In classic Stoic fashion, it's both. Let's say our neighbor's house is on fire. If you were going full Stoic, you would stand on the lawn and thank god for the challenges we have in our lives because they help us grow stronger. But their house is on fire! Stop staring at your toes and grab some buckets of water!

Stoics use, what they call, a 'reserve clause' to balance these two ways of being. We can and should help our neighbor extinguish the fire, knowing that fate may have other plans. If we try our best and do what we can and the house still burns down, we can be at peace knowing we played our part.

The Discipline of Assent

The discipline of assent is tricky to describe because to understand it, you have to know how the Stoics thought of the self. It focuses on what they call the 'true self,' which is the ultimate source of virtue.

The true self is an almost religious concept. In fact, it is often referred to as our soul. Marcus Aurelius wrote in his Meditations: "You are nothing but a little soul carrying a cadaver, as Epictetus used to say."

The true self is your rational self. It's the place

within you that gives value judgments, where your free will comes from. The reason it's relevant to the discipline of assent is its role in judgment. The three disciplines aim to guide the Stoic toward behaving correctly. How we behave follows how we think, so we should be mindful of our thoughts.

When talking about assent, we are talking about approving something. Much of your life is based on judging whether something is good, neutral, or bad. Commonly, we pursue what we consider good and avoid what we perceive as bad. The Stoics would have you take a more conscious approach to these perceptions.

Suppose you are mindful of your inner self. In that case, you can notice when you unconsciously respond to unhealthy thought patterns. Let's say you have a project you're working on, maybe a school project or something creative like music or writing. Whenever you sit down to work on it, you daydream about doing something more straightforward and fun, like video games or going to the bar. An undisciplined mind would unconsciously assent to this fantasy, drawing your attention away until you put the project down and do whatever your passions want you to do.

By becoming mindful of our true selves, we can see this process happening in its early stages, when our passion hasn't grown too large to ignore. We can nip it in the bud right then and there, saying, "Hey! I see you, the inner child of fantasy. I'm trying to get some work done. Go away!" We remove our assent and maintain our attention on the project. We become more focused, more productive, and essentially more free. We are no longer at the whims of the storm of passion. Our true self, the rational self that the Stoics believed to be above everything else within you, is again in control, and that's a good thing! In all honesty, it's the only thing we can control. Let me put all of this together for you in a way that's not so abstract.

My friend, Harvey, is an intelligent guy. We'd known each other since high school and ended up going to different colleges, but we got in touch every so often. Things seemed to be going well during the first couple of years of college. He was in a fraternity, got invited to all kinds of parties, and had what seemed to be an infinite number of friends. But in the summer of our second year, we were both back home visiting family around the same time. We got together to catch up, and something caught me totally off guard; Harvey looked ROUGH. Here was a guy just barely into his twenties, and he had bags the size of golf balls beneath his eyes. Crow's feet were already starting to form, and his palpable tiredness made me sad just looking at the guy.

After talking briefly, I finally asked what was wrong,

and he broke down. Apparently, he was failing his classes, his parents were threatening to cut him off, and he was worried he was starting to develop a drinking problem. I felt sorry for him. It seemed like he had it all going for him.

At that time, I'd been bringing Stoicism into my life and had seen positive changes. I told him how I handled the transition to adulthood with its ideas, and he perked up. To be fair, I think he would have walked on broken glass if he thought it would help him get out of this mess.

To the best of my ability, I explained the three disciplines. About how living a happy life results from being more engaged with how you think about the world. It was enough to catch his interest. I told him about some of my favorite books on Stoicism and wished him the best as we both went back to college for the fall.

I didn't see him again until after we had graduated, and the difference was immediately noticeable. He didn't go on to become valedictorian or anything, but he graduated with a good GPA, had a job lined up for him after graduation, and he generally just smiled more than the last time I saw him.

I asked him if he had read any of the books I recommended, and he put his hand on my shoulder and thanked me, saying that he had and had worked hard to bring the ideas to life. He said he no longer felt like he was chasing something he didn't understand and felt lighter because of it.

Seeing the positive effect that Stoicism has had in my life and the lives of those around me is one of the main reasons I set out to write this book. If I want to act for the betterment of all humanity, what better way than to share the ideas that have helped so many people? I've seen firsthand the benefits it provides. I hope you will, too.

Journal Prompts

Zeno's Resilience and Personal Setbacks

Zeno experienced a significant setback when his ship sank, resulting in a massive financial loss. Instead of succumbing to despair, he used the experience as a catalyst for personal growth, eventually founding Stoicism. Reflect on a major setback or challenge you've faced in your own life. How did you initially react? In hindsight, did this event lead to any personal growth or new perspectives? How can you apply Stoic principles to future challenges?

The Illusion of Material Satisfaction

The Stoics, as highlighted by Marcus Aurelius, believed that true happiness does not stem from material possessions. Think about a time you yearned for a material possession, believing it would bring you happiness. Did the joy last? Were you soon looking for the next thing? How can adopting the Stoic mindset of "amor fati" (love of one's fate) help you find contentment in what you have now?

The Three Disciplines and Personal Application

The Stoics propose three disciplines for living a good life: the discipline of desire (acceptance), the discipline of action, and the discipline of assent. Which of these disciplines do you feel you most embody daily? Which do you find most challenging? Write about specific instances where you successfully practiced one of these disciplines and moments where you struggled.

Community and Happiness

According to the chapter, achieving true happiness requires engaging with the community and maintaining natural relations. Think about your current relationship with your community. How do you actively contribute to its well-being? Are there areas where you can be more involved or show more love towards fellow human beings? Reflect on your community's role in your happi-

ness and how you can further integrate the Stoic principle of loving engagement for mutual benefit.

THREE
THE MAIN MINDSET: KEEP CALM AND CARRY ON

> "Living virtuously is equal to living in accordance with one's experience of the actual course of nature."
>
> CHRYSIPPUS

Stoicism isn't just a helping hand for the lost and confused. Many of the world's most successful entrepreneurs use Stoicism as a template for living up to their highest potential. Warren Buffet, Jeff Bezos, and Elon Musk are the easy examples. Many people trying to emulate their success look to their mindset for inspiration. It's why biographies are so popular and why people love hearing industry titans give speeches.

Well, you're in luck because if there's one thing these people have in common, it's a love and appreciation of Stoicism as a guiding hand. It is one of the reasons Stoicism is seeing such an explosion of interest lately.

We've already talked about the three disciplines, but let's get into something even more core to the Stoic mindset: virtue. Or rather, virtues. Four, to be exact. The four cardinal virtues are courage, wisdom, justice, and temperance. These four virtues were the only highest good humankind could hope to embody. Without them, pursuing the good life was nothing but a fool's errand.

Let's take a closer look at each of them.

Courage

Courage is the virtue of following through when you would rather run away. If you live long enough, you'll get more than your fair share of uncomfortable or frightening experiences. Courage is what helps us stand tall in the face of these difficult moments.

It doesn't have to be anything significant. Maybe you're arguing with a loved one, feeling nervous about a job interview, or feeling the pressure of not making enough money. None of these moments are necessarily life-altering, but they are the meat and bones of real life.

When we live courageously, we can acknowledge the unpleasantness of what we are experiencing without using it as an excuse not to show up. If courage had a slogan, it would be "Show Up!" Nobody gets a free pass through life, untarnished by challenges and sorrows.

If you really want to succeed at living well, plan on hardship being a given. You will have a bad time if your whole life plan is built for a leisurely stroll down a lazy river. I hate to be the bearer of bad news, but it's just not going to work out that way. If life was easy, why would anyone be talking about Stoicism anyway? There certainly wouldn't be any need for virtue, let alone courage.

Another vital point about courage is that it isn't just a one-off act. If you are living with courage, it's not as if you can switch it on when you need to save someone from choking and then return to enjoying your dinner. Courage is a sustained note of "Show Up!" that runs through everything you do.

Working a tedious job? Courage keeps you from quitting in favor of mooching off your family or friends. Courage is the lion's roar in your heart that says you can do so much more, pushing you to find a more positive culture to surround yourself with to pursue your dreams.

As with all of these virtues, the real-world application varies quite a bit. If you are looking for specific directions, virtue isn't that helpful. Courage in one situation may say to leave; in another, it may say to stay. The concept is universal; its application is best understood case-by-case. It's more of a subjective art than an objective science.

In the words of Epictetus, "Circumstances don't make the man; they only reveal him to himself."

Wisdom

Wisdom is probably the most enigmatic of the virtues. It's a difficult concept to understand and even harder to embody. The Stoics thought a truly wise man only came around every 500 years. Later Stoics considered wisdom more of an accumulation than a one-off accomplishment. Still, it just goes to show how highly they thought of wisdom.

Some Stoics would describe wisdom as divine and human knowledge, but that isn't all that of a helpful definition. Others would describe it as the knowledge of good and evil, but this doesn't hit the mark either. Wisdom has many dimensions.

If you embody the virtue of wisdom, you know just what to do at all times. When you pick up a pencil, you know how to hold it. Perfect wisdom would allow you to approach every situation in life as straightforwardly as picking up a pencil; you know how to do it.

Nobody is born knowing how to hold a pencil, but once you see, you don't ever really forget. You go through life from then on as a capable pencil-holder. Someone who has become wise no longer stresses themselves out about this or that ice cream flavor, nor do they spend sleepless nights worrying about others' opinions of them and their circumstances. They walk straight ahead, confident in their ability to approach the situation correctly, no matter the circumstances.

Of course, this is the ideal and not necessarily a good depiction of reality. I'm sure very wise people still have doubts and second-guess themselves. It is almost inhuman not to, which goes against the purpose of the philosophy.

If you wanted to break down what wisdom looks like from the outside, you could describe it as being resourceful, intelligent, and understanding. But unfortunately, knowing what wisdom looks like doesn't help you achieve it in your own life. You may know what bread looks and tastes like, but you will struggle to make it yourself without a recipe and an ingredient list.

You may have heard something called the prayer for serenity before. It goes like this:

> *God, grant me the serenity to accept the things I cannot change, the courage to change the things I can, and the wisdom to know the difference.*

Stoic wisdom is this knowing. It isn't the type of knowledge you could use to make a million dollars, invent the next technological breakthrough, or get an A in your history class. You could call it foundational knowledge as opposed to practical knowledge. On a boat, wisdom is the compass, not the paddle.

Justice

Justice reminds me of a man with a strong jawline, standing impossibly straight, holding an old piece of paper called THE LAW tightly against his puffed-up chest. Marcus Aurelius considered justice the source of the other three virtues. It makes sense if you think about it. As a virtue, justice has to do with how we treat others. If we live justly, we are looking out for the people around us, being honest, not stealing, aiming for the highest good of all humanity, not just getting what's ours.

If we want the best for other people, then we must be the best version of ourselves, right? It would be challenging to be lacking in other areas of your life while still managing to live a just life. It requires that we attend to our other virtues.

Let's take it a step further and consider that the other virtues might not be possible without justice. Would it be likely to be courageous while you hope for bad things to happen to your neighbor? Maybe, but your courage would be pretty damaged in the process.

The tricky thing about justice is that it feels easily hidden. Most people aren't going around professing goodwill to all humanity. People might start looking at you funny if you did. So even if you live justly, it's not immediately apparent to the people around you.

We may not always notice when people live justly, but we definitely notice when they live unjustly. It's a mystery we may never understand that good deeds often go unnoticed while bad ones stand stark. Perhaps a better way of phrasing it would be to say that justice is subtle. One just action may not get your loved ones out on the street praising your name, but acting justly all day will radiate an undeniable warmth to those around you. It starts small, as all good things do.

Temperance

Temperance may sound boring, but it is actually one of my favorites. The universe works in a balance. Nothing exists in isolation. Everything, both physical and mental, is connected to its surroundings. If it begins to take up too much space or atrophies away into nothing, the universe responds in kind.

In this sense, temperance is moderation. Psychologically, we are made up of many different pieces. We have our curious side, our creative side, and our melancholic side. Suppose we focus on one to the exclusion of the others. In that case, we drown out aspects of ourselves that should be expressed and appreciated. We may not necessarily like those aspects of ourselves, but stuffing them down makes us weaker, not stronger.

Temperance has other meanings as well. To the original Stoics, it meant something more like self-discipline or self-control, especially regarding volatile emotions. Anger, desire, and fear are valuable emotions but can become harmful if allowed too much room to grow.

Let's say you are driving to an important meeting when someone rear-ends you. You're late for the meeting, and your car is damaged. That sucks. A mind lacking self-discipline would allow their anger to flow freely at the other driver. Maybe anger from different parts of their life would join in on the opportunity to express themselves. They would feel fear about the missed meeting, conjuring all kinds of horrible outcomes because they aren't there. And so on.

None of this would happen if you lived with the virtue of temperance. You could handle the situation appropriately and move on with your day. You could call ahead at the office and let them know what happened. You would deal with the other driver with respect, knowing that accidents happen.

Our world today doesn't value temperance, at least not as much as it used to. We live in a society of big emotions. If you're happy, you're ecstatic. If you're sad, there's a river of tears at your feet. Dampening your emotional life often comes across as unhealthy, repressive, or dull.

Like the rest of the virtues, it's not all that straightforward. Many people choose to stay on the emotional rollercoaster that is their life for fear of being too ordinary, making them sick. Other people do the opposite and repress everything in favor of the logical and emotionless. Temperance should be somewhere in the middle. It's up to you to figure out what level works for you.

Each of the four virtues plays off the others. You can't have only one; they come as a package. You will be misshapen if you work to make yourself wise but lack courage. And vice versa. The lucky thing is that you are practicing them all by practicing one. This talk of virtue is fine and all, but, for being a down-to-earth philosophy, it's a bit abstract. I mean, do we decide to be wise, and that's that? If only it were that easy!

Principles of Stoicism

At the risk of sounding like a powdered wig, we grow virtue by living according to principles. Ten of them, to be exact. These principles are like guidelines that remind us of what we are attempting to accomplish and prod us along the path to Stoic sagehood. They aren't in any particular order, by the way. Being at the top of the list isn't better than being at the bottom.

THE FIRST PRINCIPLE is to live in agreement with nature. No, you don't need to walk around barefoot to do this one. Think of it like this: a mosquito is a mosquito and is expected to live the life of a mosquito; the same goes for a tree or a rock. As a human being, you would do well to live as a human being.

What does it mean to live as a human being? That is a difficult question to answer, but it meant living as a rational being for the Stoics. What differentiates us from plants and other animals is that we are rational.

We can foresee our death, make tools, be aware of our own existence, and have complex language. Many things make us unique in the universe. This book is a good example. Dolphins don't have books.

In terms of practicing this principle, think of it this way. A bear is captive to its emotions; a human doesn't need to be. By living rationally, we live according to our nature. On this point, Epictetus once said, "When our actions are combative, mischievous, angry, and rude, do we not fall away and become wild beasts?" We are not wild beasts and shouldn't act like one.

On a more human level If you are a mechanic, live as a mechanic. Don't moan about your life as a mechanic or drag your feet on the way to your job. Accept your place in the universe and apply yourself to the task given to you with all of your mind.

THE SECOND PRINCIPLE is *amor fati*. This has to do with acceptance, keeping your head held high in the face of adversity. Instead of groaning about all the ways life isn't giving you what you want, living with amor fati means accepting your life for what it is. Having gratitude for the challenges that will inevitably cross your path is a great way to keep the upper hand.

Let's say you start trading cryptocurrency, hoping to strike it rich. The only problem is you don't know what you're doing, and suddenly you've got fifty dollars in your bank account, and your credit card is maxed out.

Not going to lie; that sucks. But instead of letting this setback dictate your mental state for the next six months, you could accept the challenge for what it is. You can use this opportunity to get creative about how you will make that money back. Maybe that will lead you to a fulfilling career you hadn't considered before.

Even if you don't believe it to be accurate at first, an excellent way to ease into this mindset is to act as if everything that happens to you is put there to help guide you to your highest potential. So, in the crypto-currency example, now you're broke and feeling ashamed that you were so careless. Ask yourself, "How do I use this to grow?"

If you live with a positive mindset, your life gets better. Things don't necessarily get less complicated, but those complications feel lighter when you see they lead to good things. Suppose you remind yourself to love your fate regularly until it becomes ingrained in your worldview. In that case, you'll be amazed by the difference it makes. I promise.

. . .

THE THIRD PRINCIPLE is to understand what you can and cannot control. This is one of the most fundamental concepts in Stoicism because it gives you the psychological leverage you need to take back your mind. Sound too good to be true? Let me explain.

With amor fati, we learn to accept and appreciate our fate. One way to think about fate is that they are the things that happen to you that you don't have a say in. Funny enough, we are inferior judges of what we do and don't have control over. Many of us are anxious about how our actions will affect us. The reality is that we control very little about what happens. At an extreme level, we might say we have no control over anything except what's in our minds.

By differentiating what we do and don't have control over, we can more readily accept our circumstances. If acceptance is the opposite of resistance, then we get something when we stop resisting it. It is much easier to stop fighting if we acknowledge that something is out of our control.

To put it more concretely, let's say you just lost your job through no fault of your own. The economy took a downturn, and layoffs were inevitable. If you are under the impression that you are in control of this situation, you may plead with HR to give you your job back. You may go home and sink into depression because you have failed your family. And so on. But if you accept that this was out of your control and there is nothing you could have done to change it, then there is no one to blame, least of all yourself.

You have freed up a considerable chunk of your mental bandwidth to tackle the problem head-on instead of wasting energy fighting to let you keep your job. Roll with the punches. It hurts less.

THE FOURTH PRINCIPLE is to live by virtue. Orient your life to the four cardinal virtues; you will never lose your way again. Be diligent in applying Stoic ethics to truly receive its benefits. Be courageous. Be just and wise and temperate. You will truly understand the good life once you use these values. They are the highest possible good we can attain. It's okay to falter, but always get back up and try again.

THE FIFTH PRINCIPLE IS DISCERNMENT. It would help if you learned to distinguish between the good, the bad, and the neutral. We have already talked quite a bit about the good. These are the four virtues.

The Stoics considered the four vices to be the bad: folly, injustice, cowardice, and indulgence.

You may have noticed that the four vices are the opposite of the four virtues. If you are the opposite of wise, you are foolish. If you are not just, you are at risk of being unjust. Of course, the world is not as black and white as all that, which leaves us with the neutral, sometimes called the indifferent.

The interesting thing about the indifferent is that it also includes health and sickness, wealth and poverty, and life and death. These things do not have inherent moral value, either positive or negative. The value of health is relative to the situation and, therefore, neutral.

If a serial killer is in good health, that is not really a net good. We would prefer he were too sick to harm anyone. As a stoic, our job is to learn to discern what is good and bad.

THE SIXTH PRINCIPLE is to take action. We are here learning about Stoicism to learn how to live well. The whole point of a philosophy of life is to have practical answers to real-world problems. If we are learning how to behave, perceive and analyze, and do nothing with that knowledge, then it is safe to say that we have wasted our time.

If it is nothing else, Stoicism is a philosophy of action. We are meant to apply this wisdom to our actual lives. It does not give us metaphysical answers to life's grand questions; it gives us actionable insight.

THE SEVENTH PRINCIPLE is to practice misfortune. We should regularly tell ourselves that whatever can go wrong will. What an idea, I know! If you've ever heard of the concept of anti-fragility, you may already know where this is going. When modern medicine aims to rid people of an allergy, they give them small doses of what they are allergic to. We provide them with that virus when we want to inoculate them against it. When we want to build our muscles up, we tear them down. If we give ourselves small doses of imagined misfortune, we are better at adapting to actual misfortune. The crucial part of this is not to become pessimistic, but indifferent. We are attempting to build stability through what is sometimes called 'negative visualization.'

For example, let's say we have just started a new business. We then visualize our business failing, not through the lens of fear but through the lens of acceptance. We do not hope for it to happen; we do not lay awake at night in fear of it happening. We accept the possibility that things will go wrong, and when the business fails, we are ready to learn from our mistakes and try again.

THE EIGHTH PRINCIPLE is to add a reserve clause to your actions. We've already touched on this briefly before. We accept our fate but don't let acceptance act as an excuse for inaction.

For example, we are sitting at a restaurant, and someone begins to choke. Accepting fate entirely might mean that we accept that that person will die. Obviously, there are better things to do than this. Instead, we should try to save them, knowing that fate may have other plans. If we fail, at least we try. Action and acceptance are then able to exist in the same space.

THE NINTH PRINCIPLE is to turn obstacles into opportunities. Another way to think about this principle is: take control of your perceptions. The Stoics taught that your perception of events is the only thing you have control over. The outside world is almost always classified under the indifferent/neutral category. It's how we perceive these differences that matter.

So something neutral happens. We get in a car accident and break our leg. Ouch. If our perception of the situation turns negative, we indulge in needless self-harm. Instead, think of how you can make the most of the situation. You can't go to work for a few weeks while you recover. You now have time to work on that hobby you're always saying you're too busy for. Congratulations, you now have some free time. It's that easy to do, and you wouldn't believe how much better your life becomes.

THE TENTH and final principle is mindfulness. We don't often associate mindfulness with philosophy. We usually think of Buddhism or yoga. But Stoic mindfulness is a crucial part of the program. How can we expect to take control of our minds if we are not mindful?

For those who are only vaguely familiar with mindfulness, you're not alone. It's a vague term that describes everything from being empathetic to eating healthy. In this context, mindfulness is the learned capacity to be fully aware. When we are mindful, we pay attention to our thoughts, feelings, and actions, both big and small. We can't expect to make meaningful changes if we aren't paying attention to our minds.

The Payoff and a Reminder

Alright, so you've been downloading the user manual on Stoicism this whole chapter, and you're bored thinking, "That sounds like a lot of work. Why not just ignore it and do whatever I want?" You could. Sure, but you'd be giving up all the beautiful benefits that Stoicism has been shown to provide.Here are some examples.

Do you suffer from social anxiety? Stoicism has been known to help with that. Do you struggle staying focussed? Stoicism can help with that as well.

Clearing the mental clutter is a great way to kick into high gear. Through mindfulness, you can decrease how distracted you get, slow down the mental chatter, and train your brain by directing your attention. Ultimately, the goal is to achieve peace of mind. A calm, contentedness that carries you through any day, no matter how difficult. That's eudaimonia. That's the goal and the purpose behind Stoicism. It's yours if you want it. You just have to follow through.

The hardest part about following through is remembering to follow through. That's why I'm a big believer in reminders. Some people get tattoos, and some people set reminders on their phones. As for me, I like physical objects, so I designed this poster that you can print out and hang somewhere you'll see throughout the day.

The aim of the poster isn't to introduce new ideas so much as to quickly remind you that you are working to build up a strong sense of character in yourself. The medium matters less than the method, so if you think of another way to remind yourself that's better for you; no hard feelings. Go for it!

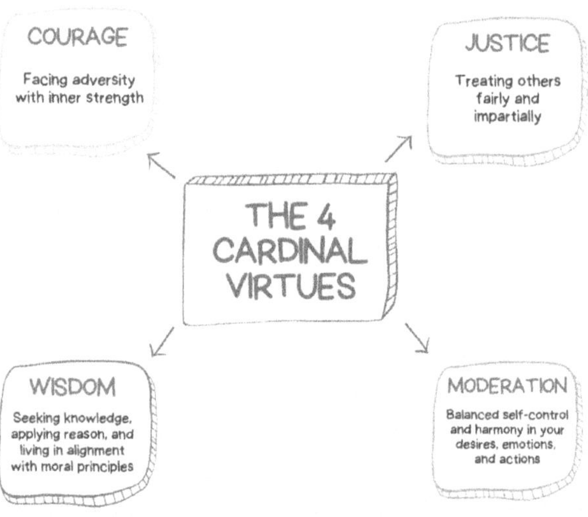

Journal Prompts

Reflecting on the Four Cardinal Virtues

Consider the Stoic virtues of courage, wisdom, justice, and temperance. How have they appeared in your life? Think about moments when you've embodied these virtues and times you might not have. How can you integrate them more deeply into your daily decisions and behaviors?

The Role of Stoicism in Modern Success

Prominent figures like Warren Buffet, Jeff Bezos, and Elon Musk are said to value Stoicism. Do you believe Stoicism contributes to their achievements? Reflect on your personal definition of success and its alignment with Stoic principles. Would embracing Stoic virtues reshape your measure of success? If so, how?

Embracing Stoic Principles in Daily Life

The chapter introduces ten core Stoic principles,

such as living in agreement with nature, amor fati, discerning control, and practicing misfortune, among others. Reflect on a recent challenging situation you encountered. How could these principles have influenced your response or perception of the situation? Identify three principles that could have been particularly relevant, and explore how integrating them has changed your experience.

Stoicism and Personal Well-being

Stoicism promises several benefits, including reduced social anxiety, increased focus, and a deep-seated calm. Think about areas in your life where you feel the need for growth or balance. How might Stoic teachings and mindfulness assist in addressing these areas? Envision a version of your life where you actively apply these principles and describe the changes you anticipate in your mental state and daily actions.

FOUR
HOW CAN STOICISM HELP WITH STRESS AND ANXIETY?

"Today, I escaped anxiety. Or no, I discarded it because it was within me, in my own perceptions — not outside."

MARCUS AURELIUS

Stress and anxiety plague modern society. I would bet good money that there isn't a single person alive today who doesn't experience anxiety or personally know someone who experiences anxiety. It's the most common mental illness, affecting roughly one-third of the world's population. So if you know two people, odds are one of you has it. This chapter will discuss the common problems of stress and anxiety and how Stoicism addresses them. But let's make sure we're on the same page first.

What is Stress?

According to the World Health Organization, stress is "a state of worry or mental tension caused by a difficult situation."

Stress feels obvious, but we're often better at noticing it in others than ourselves. When it's depicted on television, you may see someone carrying a lot of papers, dropping pens and coffee, and running in three different directions at once. Real life isn't quite so dramatic, and the symptoms of stress aren't always this visible, but the idea isn't too far off. You can think of stress as feeling overwhelmed, like there isn't enough time in the day to get everything done or that the task at hand is more than you can handle. For most people, this will be a by-product of their job or work.

There's a reason we hear about stress so often. For one, it's widespread. According to the American Institute of Stress, 55% of Americans are stressed daily. The global average is 35%, making the United States one of the most stressed-out countries in the world. We also hear about it so often because it is a silent killer. Chronic stress can cause significant health problems. Science has shown that 75-90% of all diseases are stress-related. Take a second to think about that statistic for a second.

Stress will manifest differently for different people, but common, recognizable symptoms exist. We often separate these symptoms into three categories: physical, mental, and behavioral.

Physical Symptoms

In the transition to a new job several years ago, I encountered the physical impact of anxiety. My body seemed to echo the worries my mind kept replaying at the idea of moving from a comfortable role to an entirely different industry. Insomnia was the first sign, with sleepless nights becoming the norm. I'd toss and turn, kept up by racing thoughts. This insomnia led to chronic fatigue; I was perpetually drained, shrouded in a fog of exhaustion that no amount of caffeine could clear.

Muscle tension soon followed. Anticipation and uncertainty took the form of tight knots in my neck and back. It felt like I was carrying my anxieties on my shoulders. My skin started breaking out in acne, reminiscent of my teenage years.

The experience taught me how intertwined my physical health is with my mental state, reminding me of the importance of finding equilibrium in both, especially in times of change.

Mental Symptoms

Not only does stress manifest as physical symptoms, it often hijacks your cognitive abilities. Mental symptoms of stress include depression, anxiety, irritability, lack of focus, and restlessness. One way to think about stress is that your brain is frying. You've pushed it past its limits of optimal functionality, and it's starting to break down. The mental fog descends, making it nearly impossible to see past the haze. Tasks that used to feel like second nature suddenly require herculean effort. It's like trying to run a marathon through quicksand. You find yourself constantly losing things, forgetting important dates, and even fundamental decision-making feels challenging. This cognitive impairment only adds to the distress, creating a vicious cycle that feels almost impossible to escape. My mind does all these things when it's not functioning right. It's the world's worst emotional cocktail, believe me.

Behavioral Symptoms

As for behavior, chronic stress often leads to drug and alcohol abuse, eating too much or too little, and generally forgoing personal care. If you're stressed out and have been for a while, you're less likely to exercise regularly and more likely to isolate yourself. For being so common, stress really packs a punch. I'm not trying to scare you. Some stress is normal, downright unavoidable, really. Experiencing occasional stressful situations or feelings of stress isn't going to cause these symptoms. When we experience chronic, sustained stress, our health begins to deteriorate.

What really stands out about stress is that it is perfectly designed to fly under the radar. Everyone deals with stress (making it easy to ignore), and its symptoms are secondary (making it easy to miss). What I mean by secondary is that stress itself doesn't commonly have apparent symptoms like a rash on your arm. If you touch poison ivy, you have a rash that looks and itches like poison ivy. It's obvious. If you are having trouble sleeping, are drinking too much alcohol, and are suffering from headaches, it's not that obvious those things are due to your highly demanding job.

This is why part of stress management is learning how to identify symptoms of stress in your body and mind. We'll talk more about how to manage your stress in a second. But first, let's talk about stress' close relative: anxiety.

What is Anxiety?

Anxiety is similar to stress in several ways. The first is that both anxiety and stress are natural, everyday phenomena. Our bodies have developed stress and anxiety to keep us alive. Sometimes, anxiety and stress go a bit overboard, though. Fear is an excellent example of this.

Feeling fear is not pleasant, but it serves a purpose. Nobody should be afraid all of the time. That's unhealthy. However, you would get into much trouble if you never felt fear. You'd go out and take selfies with grizzly bears, jump off of cruise ships in the middle of the night on a dare, or drive a motorcycle at night with your lights off.

None of those scenarios are going to end well for you, and fear is the thing that helps you understand that. In an ideal setting, anxiety is the mental process that enables you to anticipate threats.

A zebra who notices a rustling in the tall grass will become anxious that a lion will jump out and eat them.

It will then use that unpleasant feeling as motivation to move to a new area, possibly saving its life.

I can't speak for everyone, but most people aren't being hunted down by predators these days. That doesn't stop our brain from doing what it's developed to do: protect us from danger. That means we still experience anxiety even though the environment that anxiety was 'built for' doesn't exist anymore.

Anxiety is still helpful in modern industrial society. For example, it keeps us alert on the road. For many, the feeling has grown to encompass situations it was not designed for. When that happens, anxiety stops being a regular, functional level of worry and threatens to become debilitating.

Anxiety becomes an anxiety disorder when the fear and worry you are experiencing begin to negatively affect how you go about your day. In other words, if your quality of life decreases due to your anxiety, it's gone too far. Excessive fear, panic attacks, and muscle tension are all common symptoms of anxiety gone awry. Someone experiencing this may find themselves avoiding certain activities or social situations out of worry.

Some people view being overly anxious as something integral to their personality. That it is incurable.That we should be proud of our anxiety taking over our lives.

Moving forward, we will be operating under the idea that this isn't true. I am not a doctor, but the tools we discuss will likely help if you suffer from debilitating anxiety. Still, they should not be a replacement for a medical professional.

If your goal is never to experience anxiety again, I'm sorry, but that's impossible. I'm not peddling a fantasy here. Anxiety is a normal part of life, like pain or ice cream. You are more likely to never see another ice cream cone than to never experience anxiety again. Personally, I'm not sure which I would prefer...

As a recap, we aren't trying to eradicate anxiety from our lives; we're trying to learn how to live with it healthily. Most everyone has heard of stress management. Anxiety management is just as important. Let's talk about how Stoicism can help us with both.

Slaying Stress & Anxiety

Learning how to regulate our emotions should be included in our education system. Still, most of us have to figure it out on our own. Lucky for us, there are many resources for people looking to understand how to live in a balanced, healthy way. For some, that might mean therapy. For others, reading philosophy or psychology books like this one is enough. People should do what works for them. Whether people realize it or not,

Stoicism has significantly influenced this field, including (as I mentioned earlier) providing the foundation for Cognitive Behavioral Therapy. We aren't going into a full explanation of CBT or how it works, but suppose you're skeptical of what's being offered here. In that case, it's good to know that these ideas have stood the test of time and continue influencing how we approach positive psychology.

Mindfulness

The first and most fundamental concept to start us off is Stoic mindfulness. If you haven't learned to be mindful, you will find the rest of these tools pretty challenging. It would be like trying to skateboard blind. It's been done before, but it will be easier if you open your eyes. We've already talked about mindfulness, so I won't spend much time on it here. Still, as a refresher, mindfulness is what allows you to notice the subtle mental happenings that are going on in your brain. We can be more precise in our habits and exercises by paying attention to what our mind is doing.

We can then start with one of Stoicism's central concepts: change what you can control and accept what you can't. This idea seems ideally suited to address anxiety. If you have a job interview coming up that's causing an unhealthy amount of stress, reminding yourself of this maxim could be just the exercise you need to face your fears. You can't control the person who interviews you. You don't get to decide if you get the job or not. The only thing you do have control over is yourself. Suppose you pivot your focus away from the aspects you have no control over and begin to focus on the variables you control. In that case, you'll notice your anxiety starts to ease up. This is a simple explanation of a complicated and sometimes messy mental exercise, but the reward is well worth it. It can apply to any situation you may find yourself in, so don't be afraid to experiment with it when you use it. If things begin to feel overwhelming, try to identify what exactly you are worried about and then ask yourself if it's something you have control over. If not, take a leap of faith and accept that you will receive the best possible outcome for you. Even if it isn't the outcome you wanted.

Negative Visualization

This next one is going to sound a little funny. I want you to practice negative visualization. That's right, one way the Stoics discovered you could conquer your stress and anxiety is to imagine all the worst-case scenarios and then visualize them happening. Sounds like a bad trip, am I right? Actually, I'm wrong. Although it's not the best party trick, visualizing things going wrong prepares us for the real possibility that they will go wrong. And if they do, it's no sweat because we've already confronted our fears.

For example, let's say you are in an internship and working on a big project. You want everyone to be impressed by how smart, talented, and creative you are. Only now, you're staying up until 3 am, perfecting every little detail and drinking too much coffee; thinking why is my leg numb, and where is my mind? Talk about stress! All that mental pressure is really taking its toll. It may feel like you're doing a good job, but you'd be doing much better if you just relaxed. How do you do that? Take a second out of your day and think about what you are worried will go wrong about this project. Be specific and thorough.

Now visualize how that will play out and be honest. In one scenario, your boss is unhappy with your performance and tells you so. The dramatic version would be him standing with his fists on his desk, shouting obscenities at you. At the same time, spit ejects from his lips and onto your already tear-streaked face. The realistic version would be that he pulls you aside and gives you some constructive criticism, calmly explaining which areas need more attention the next time. The second version doesn't sound so bad. I guess you can relax a little.

Do that for each scenario you can come up with, and you'll realize that your fear of the situation is mainly self-generated. This is what we've been saying all along, that your perception of the problem is the metaphorical engine that drives your emotional state. If it's running correctly, it won't overheat, and it won't make strange noises.

By practicing negative visualization, we are calibrating our perception of reality. It's not a perfect machine. It needs to be tuned up sometimes. That's why checking in with yourself regularly is essential to ensure that your perception of the world correlates with what you are actually experiencing. If it doesn't, you're staging yourself into a story that's not fun and not helpful.

Do Something

Here's one that's less cerebral: Do something. Go to the gym, cook a good meal, write in a journal, learn how to fingerpaint, make a fun video, swim in a river, read a book; just do something. I don't know if you've heard the phrase "idle hands do the devil's work." Well, that's not Stoicism, but it illustrates my point: your mind wants stimulation, and if you don't give it what it wants, it will start to create its own.

Also, getting active is a great way to relieve tension. As I said before, one of the symptoms of stress and anxiety is that your body tenses up. It's as if it's bottling up all that negativity and storing it inside, like one of those hoarders you see on TV. Throw it out! Take all that nasty mental waste and chuck it out the window by doing something fun and healthy. Ride a bike, go on a hike, or even learn how to play the harp. If you're feeling stuck, the inertia of your mental slumber will be the hardest part. Pick something that sounds mildly interesting and take the first step. In the words of Seneca, "The whole future lies in uncertainty: live immediately."

Memento Mori

Speaking of the future, the Stoics also had a slogan that is our next exercise for slaying stress: memento mori. This translates as 'remember death.' Like many Stoic exercises, this seems counterintuitive, but it's a fairly common idea. You've probably heard it in its more modern phrasing, 'life is short...' followed by some romantic appeal to living life to the fullest. 'Life is short, don't forget to stop and smell the roses.' That sort of thing. The concept is the same, really.

The Stoics say that we should remind ourselves every so often that there is only one thing sure in life: that we will die. When we do this, we aren't falling into a morbid fascination with our death. We are trying to keep ourselves from falling into mindless routines. It can be easy as the years pass by to become complacent. We may have nestled into a comfortable lifestyle, and there doesn't seem to be much reason to rally ourselves out of it. The problems we could address today can always be put off until tomorrow. The dreams we had for ourselves are too far off, and who knows if we would ever even achieve them. Better to set them down until the conditions are just right to begin.

The Stoics would remind you that your death is inevitable and could happen at any moment. It's better to do something while the heart still beats if something needs doing. If there's something you want to accomplish, you're better off doing it now while you have the chance.

So, memento mori can remind us to stay on top of our lives. It's also a reminder to let go of things that aren't worth holding on to. If this were our last day on earth, would we really want to spend it stressing about some small thing that happened at work? If it sounds like a poor use of your last day, then it stands to reason that it's a poor use of any day.

I've noticed that people who regularly practice memento mori talk about its positive impact on their lives. They often feel more grateful for the opportunities they've been given and the people around them. They feel a sense of wonder at the beauty that surrounds us. Knowing that everything will all go away one day helps you see the world with fresh eyes. We get a new lease on life, as they say. As Marcus Aurelius says, "This is the mark of perfection of character—to spend each day as if it were your last, without frenzy, laziness, or any pretending."

Putting It Into Practice

This is all well and good, but it's a lot easier to say these things than do them, believe me. You may be reading this thinking it would be nice to bring these ideas into your life, but you may be a bit lost about how it works. If we were in control of our minds already, we wouldn't need these concepts, right? That's why it's so crucial to start at the basics. We must build the foundation before we can start working on the house. Let's start building.

Mindful Activities

We've already discussed mindfulness, but how do we actually do it? Repetition, repetition, repetition. Only by carving out the mental pathways can we introduce mindfulness meaningfully.

Suppose we want the full benefits of mindfulness. In that case, we need to bring it into every possible moment until it becomes habitual, and we don't even need to think about it. We can practice it while we're driving our car, while we are eating, working, gardening, or exercising.

Go for a Walk

Let's take walking as an example of how this is done. As you are walking, you want to focus on the present moment and feel the sensation of walking. The pressure on your feet, the movement of your joints, the breath through your nose. We can't notice all of it at once; our attention doesn't work that way, so we can calmly focus on one aspect at a time.

The purpose is to settle our minds. Very often, especially in the digital age, our minds move at lightning speed. We dart from one activity to the next. We mentally move so fast that we barely even register our experiences. We are instead living in some strange mental landscape, harassed by anxiety and only rarely grounding ourselves in the physical.

Listen to Music

One of my favorite ways to practice mindfulness is by listening to music. Some people call this 'deep listening,' but that's a high-brow way of saying you're paying attention. Don't multitask, don't do anything except sit and listen.

One way to think about mindfulness is that it strengthens our ability to control the focus of our attention, and music is something fun to focus on. While focusing on the music, try to register how it affects all of your senses. Music is auditory, but we also register it through our sense of touch. How does your body feel as the music changes? Do you tense up at parts? Is the music tugging at your emotions?

Meditation

We often associate meditation with mindfulness, and for a good reason. When we meditate, we are using mindfulness to turn the focus of our attention on ourselves. We become the object of our attention.

Meditating makes us calmer, more aware, capable, focused, less stressed, and anxious, and we treat ourselves better the more we get to know ourselves. If we are a machine, meditation is the process of re-engineering. We pull ourselves apart piece by piece and look at how all these different things make up 'us.' If you go really far in meditation, you can attempt to discover your true self. At least, that's what spiritual meditators call it. You can call it whatever you want, but the process is the same. You realize you have an arm, but you are not your arm. You have thoughts, but you are not thoughts. Who are you? Where are you in this body and mind? It's a fascinating pursuit that I highly recommend.

But back to basics. Many of you will have never practiced meditation, even if almost everyone has heard of it. It seems weird, esoteric, and even dull. We have plenty of options for how we spend our time; why would we pick to sit still and do nothing? That's up to you, but if you're looking to decrease your stress and anxiety levels, you won't find a better tool.

The critical part of starting a meditation practice is to do just what is necessary. You wouldn't go to the gym and start an exercise routine by deadlifting 300 pounds. Start small and work your way up. We are building the muscle of our minds.

Find somewhere comfortable to sit. You can sit on a pillow, on a chair, or on your bed. You can buy fancy meditation cushions, but they aren't necessary, and you certainly don't need them. This can and should be free to try. So you're seated and in a comfortable position. Your posture is good. Now close your eyes and take a second to feel the situation. I like doing it in the morning so I don't forget, because it's part of my routine.

Ask yourself how your morning starts, not through a conversation with yourself but by listening to your body and mind. Are you tense, tired, or agitated? Do you feel energized or sluggish? There's nothing you need to do with this information. The purpose is to take a mental note of how you are feeling.

Now turn your focus to your breath. I focus on the nostrils, where I can feel the air coming in and out. Try to keep your focus on this 'in and out' of your breath. You are 100% going to lose focus. Your mind will wander. It's what your brain does, and you don't need to get upset about it. Just take your focus and reapply it to your breath. No problem. You can count if it helps you focus. Each in and out is one breath. Try counting to ten and then starting over at one. If you lose focus, start over at one. Once you're hitting ten consistently, move up to twenty. This can be an excellent way to keep track of how you are progressing.

There are lots of resources to look at if you want more details. I recommend *The Mind Illuminated* by Culadasa, aka John Yates. He's a neuroscientist and longtime meditator who very effectively breaks down the process of learning meditation. He includes the science behind it without losing the big-picture ideas involved.

Two things I'll say before we move on, though. One is that you need to make your practice consistent. I aim for five days a week. Most experts say you should do it every day. Still, having a few days off makes my practice more consistent because I don't beat myself up for missing a day. Find a rhythm and pace that works for you. Try starting at five minutes. Just five minutes of meditation, five days a week.

Remember, the goal is not to shut off your mind. You will have thoughts, and that's okay. The point isn't to make your thoughts disappear, especially at first. Treat your thoughts as something your brain tries to do while practicing, and return to the breath.

Journaling

The last practice I recommend is journaling. How to journal is pretty subjective. It's as simple as getting a journal and writing in it daily, but what you write is up to you. It's your journal, after all. I think it's safe to say that you are writing things down in such a way as to help you process your life in a healthy way. What do I mean by that?

Let's say you write in your journal at the end of your day. You write about what you did that day, how you are feeling, what you are working on, and how they are going. That's a pretty standard journal entry.

You can also work out problems in the journal. If I have an idea I am having trouble formulating, writing it down helps me to understand it better. I'm often surprised at the result.

Be bold in your exploration of yourself. You can say something really crazy, something you would never admit to another human being. Write it down and realize, wow, I think that. Is that okay? Why do I believe that? It's very liberating.

You can also write something creative as a journal entry. I often process complex emotions through writing music and lyrics. Journaling is language-based, so writing is the go-to. You can write a poem, a short story, or a song. You could also draw something if that's more your style.

You can start with any of these practices I've discussed above and build up to the others, or you can introduce all of them at once. None of them take up *too* much time. The important part is to keep doing it once you start. You won't see the benefits of any of them if you only do them once or twice and then stop.

Keep at it, and a few months later, you'll look back and think, wow, it's such a small part of my day, but I honestly feel so much better. And it's all free!

Journal Prompts

Personal Experiences with Stress and Anxiety

> *Reflect on your personal experiences with stress and anxiety. Have there been moments in your life where you felt overwhelmed, much like the author's transition to a new job? What were the physical and mental symptoms you experienced? How did these experiences affect your day-to-day life? In your reflection, consider how you've managed or coped with these feelings. Have they been effective? Why or why not? Are there patterns in your life or specific triggers that seem to exacerbate your feelings of stress and anxiety?*

Navigating Modern Stress with Stoicism

> *The author emphasizes the difference between normal stress and anxiety versus chronic or debilitating forms of these feelings. Delve deeper into your understanding of your own stress and anxiety. Are there situations or instances where these reactions are appropriate and beneficial; acting as a protective mechanism? Conversely, are there times when these feelings seem excessive or*

misaligned with the situation at hand? Consider the role of modern society in this context - do you believe that our current environment exacerbates these feelings? Reflect on how the ancient philosophy of Stoicism might provide tools or perspectives to help you navigate and manage your stress and anxiety in a contemporary setting.

Contemplating Control and Outcomes

Reflect on a recent situation where you felt significant anxiety or stress about an outcome or event. Break down the situation into factors you could control and those you couldn't. How would applying the Stoic principle of "change what you can control and accept what you can't" alter your perspective or emotional reaction to the situation? Dive deep into understanding if your emotional responses were tied more to factors within or outside of your control.

Exploring Negative Visualization

Consider an upcoming event or project that brings anxiety or unease. Practice the Stoic exercise of negative visualization by imagining the worst-case scenarios tied to this event. Be specific in detailing these outcomes. Now, contrast these imagined outcomes with more realistic, probable outcomes. Reflect on how this exercise changes your perception of the event or project. Does envisioning these scenarios make you more prepared, lessen your anxiety, or shift your focus in any way?

FIVE

STOICS ARE NOT HERMITS: FOSTERING AND NAVIGATING RELATIONSHIPS

"Nature bore us related to one another ... She instilled in us a mutual love and made us compatible ... Let us hold everything in common; we stem from a common source. Our fellowship is very similar to an arch of stones, which would fall apart if they did not reciprocally support each other."

SENECA

One of the most common misconceptions about Stoics is that they are cold and emotionless. We think of someone gray and amorphous, like a humorless wallflower. Not exactly the most romantic stereotype. Who would want to date someone like that?

It's easy to see why people have this idea. Stoicism teaches us to control our emotions and to have a steady hand. From the outside, this can look a lot like being an emotionless grouch. Suppose someone expects a passionate and volatile response and is met with calm rationality. In that case, they may wonder what's wrong with this person.

Just because someone isn't expressing an intense emotion doesn't necessarily mean they aren't experiencing it. It also doesn't mean the feeling is being repressed, although it very well could be. There is a risk of not understanding the more subtle aspects of this process, which could lead to someone repressing their feelings. That's not the goal. We aren't trying to stuff it down as far as it can go, never to be seen again.

We also aren't trying to let our emotions control our minds and make us do things we don't want. In any case, I think most Stoics understand this. We enjoy having emotions as a part of our life. They give flavor and nuance to the world.

All this is to say that Stoics are just like everybody else. They have all the same wants and needs as every other human being on the planet. If there is anything we all have in common, it's that we are social creatures. Far from making us distant and anti-social, Stoicism teaches us that much of what gives us meaning in our lives involves other people. If you think back to the four cardinal virtues, Justice is the virtue of being a positive force in the lives of others. "If you have nothing to stir you up and rouse you to action," says Seneca, "nothing which will test your resolution by its threats and hostilities; if you recline in unshaken comfort, it is not tranquility; it is merely a flat calm."

Life is not meant to be tucked away from society, wrapped in a blanket of emotional comfort. We are meant to be out there with others, working to make the world better for everyone. We don't have to become president to be a positive societal force. We start with what is around us. No matter how isolated we may feel, we need *some* contact with other people. That is the first step to becoming a force for good.

The question remains, though. What does it mean to be a force for good? How does one go about accomplishing such an ambiguous project? It's not as if there is an end goal in mind where we can stop and pat ourselves on the back, saying, "We did it. We were a force for good. Pack up the trailer; we're finished." In much the same way, a relationship is never completed. The process of building a good and healthy relationship is an ongoing one. There is no final destination, only the journey of improving incrementally every day.

The Tools of the Trade

It all starts with you. A relationship is a connection between two people. That can be your spouse, friends, family, or even the clerk at the grocery store. No matter who it's with, one-half of the connection is you.

It stands to reason that if you want to build the best relationships possible, you must ensure you are ready to make that connection. You can't control how the other person will behave or what they think. You can only show up having put in the work to be the best version of yourself.

A great place to start is by taking the time to understand your emotions and learn how to regulate them. Again, we are not repressing them. The goal is to learn what they are trying to tell us and then let them go. It's a delicate balance but certainly doable.

Think of your emotions as messengers trying to notify you of something. It could be something dangerous, or it could be something helpful. We've had emotions for as long as we've been a species. They serve a purpose.

It's worth remembering, though, that we aren't

perfect machines. Sometimes these helpful messengers can become too sensitive. Let's say a feeling of fear washes over us, warning us that our friend doesn't like our shirt. It's worth noticing that our friend doesn't like our shirt, but it probably isn't necessary to have a full-on panic attack or to break down in tears. That's why we talk about regulating our emotions. If the settings are set too high, we need to turn them down a little so we can healthily engage with the world.

Framing

Another way to express healthy emotions is through our framing. If we are experiencing a lot of negative emotions around an event, try looking at it from a different perspective. Obstacles will come. When confronted by an obstacle, we can frame it in a way that plays to our strengths. Let's say an economic recession hits. We can panic, point fingers, or throw our hands in the air if we choose. Or, if you're finding those avenues are making you unhappy, you could frame it more positively.

Instead of focusing on the negative aspects, we can weave them into a larger story. In that scenario, you could say, "Good thing I've been studying Stoicism. I feel ready to take on this challenge. Let me see if I can put my practice to good use."

By learning to regulate and express our emotions positively, we are in a much better position to uphold our half of a relationship. If we haven't learned to control our emotions, we may find that people are less willing to engage with us because we are, in effect, asking them to shoulder the burden of our emotional instability.

If our goal is to build the best possible relationships we can, we need to be able to stand on our own two feet. Most people are barely able to hold themselves up. If you're essentially asking others to carry you, you may find that many just aren't capable, and for good reason!

The flip side is if you want to be the type of person who will be there for anyone no matter what, you need to be able to hold yourself up and then some. Not only do you need to get on your feet, you need to build the emotional strength to follow through on that goal.

Control, Compassion, and Empathy

One helpful tool in that pursuit is the Stoic idea of control. I don't know about you, but a good portion of the issues I have in my relationships with people revolve around wanting them to behave in the way of my choosing. Instead, they do what they want, and I get upset.

Stoicism reminds us that many things are out of our control, and we are better off accepting them for what they are. I can choose how to react, but if I am trying to be a force for good in the life of someone I consider to be acting poorly, I need to accept who they are, both in that moment and all other moments.

It's not enough to accept them for a few minutes, and then, when they continue to behave contrary to how I want them to act, I get mad at them. That's not really acceptance; that's a tactic of persuasion.

Let's say you and a family member disagree with each other politically. You wish they wouldn't support so-and-so for president. Stoicism would say you are under the illusion of control over this person. Their beliefs aren't up to you.

Suppose you find it really upsetting and can't imagine the possibility that you could accept them because of their politics. In that case, you are not being a force for good. Instead of trying to understand the other person, you are attempting to force them to behave differently by retracting your affection for them.

Some self-reflection would serve you well in this situation. Why does it bother you so much that the other person believes what they believe? Is there any possible scenario in which their belief could be justified?

If you are recoiling in disgust at the idea of trying to understand another human being, accepting others and building common understandings between us is the Stoic way to bring goodness and virtue into society. We should build bridges, not moats.

Next, compassion and empathy are your tools. This is not the same as pity. We aren't pitying someone for thinking differently. We are trying to see through their eyes and to walk in their shoes. When we understand where someone is coming from, we are better positioned to engage with them.

You may have noticed that I am spending a lot of time discussing people we disagree with. Many people say we have isolated ourselves from people who don't think like us that we live in social bubbles that echo our worldview.

When we like people and agree with them, getting along with them is easy. It's when we disagree that most of us are at a loss for what to do. It's easier said than done, and sometimes it's better just to walk away, but I think we are too quick to do so. We should at make an effort to understand each other.

Building and Keeping Healthy Relationships

Our first encounter with relationships is with our families. Here we create the building blocks we will use to construct all future relationships. For many of us, some blocks we make will be good, and some will be bad. It's a mixed bag. We may learn compassion and responsibility while learning emotional distance and repressed sexuality. We may learn optimism and open communication while learning how to let our emotions get the better of us. We don't really get to choose what we take away from our upbringing.

Growing up, I didn't always see eye to eye with my family. Around the age of fourteen, I started to rationalize better, and I could better understand who I was in relation to who they were. I didn't like what I saw. As I've gotten older, I've been able to empathize with them more. My parents were really young when they started having children. They did their best, and I respect what they did, even if they were flawed. We all are. It doesn't bother me as much as it used to to admit this.

As I've spent more time with my family as an adult, I've grown really attached to them. My parents and siblings are lovely people. The question I'm left with is: have they changed, or have I? The truth is that I've changed. I've become more open to them, more trusting. I don't feel the need to push them away like I used to. They've also changed over the years, but I'm closer to them because I've allowed them in. I can't help but think that Stoicism has helped me grow closer to my family. I've become more tolerant of other people's imperfections because of it. I'm not as quick to assign blame or to run away when things aren't going my way.

The same thing goes for friendships. When I was younger, I was a mediocre friend. I would often criticize others for not doing things as I thought they should. I had lots of opinions about how other people should live their life. By reminding myself that I am only in charge of myself, I learned how to relax. Even if I want what's best for my friends, their actions are outside my control. As they should be. I have no right to tell them what to do. I became a better friend by applying the Stoic concept of controlling what I can and accepting what I can't.

Usually, when people say relationships, they think of romantic relationships. For good reason, too. If you're in a relationship, it is *the* relationship. Friends and family are important, but nothing compares to the interweaving connection with your partner. Your partner will see every aspect of you, given enough time. There are so many ways a relationship can turn sour. It's a delicate balancing act, and many of us aren't very good at it, but Stoicism can help us be less bad at it.

By decreasing our reactivity, we are more likely to be able to listen to what our partner is saying. By practicing mindfulness, we are more capable of understanding our own drives and desires and can then express them more clearly. We are better lovers when we are our best selves. Then there's the matter of having a solid inner foundation. Suppose we enter a relationship expecting the other person to be the primary source of our happiness and well-being. In that case, we are actually asking a lot. If we learn to place our primary foundation of joy within ourselves, we won't be putting so much of a demand on our partner, which can help.

That isn't to say we should expect our partner to not make us happy. It's a difference of degree. It's one thing to be self-sustaining and want someone to share your life with. It's another thing to get upset at your partner when your life isn't going how you want. It's a pretty nuanced issue. There's no real black and white. Put simply, when we are healthy and happy, we make better partners because we do not require them to shoulder us, on top of their own problems.

Stoicism helps us understand our values and better understand what type of person we are looking to spend our lives with. It also allows us to shrug off the small slights and disagreements that inevitably happen in relationships. Knowing how to resolve conflict healthily is helpful in our romantic lives and all areas of our life. Stoicism teaches us that most things are neither good nor bad but 'indifferent,' morally speaking. By shifting our perspective away from judging everything as good or bad, we free ourselves of emotional reactivity.

In terms of conflict, we may want a particular outcome. Still, by reminding ourselves of amor fati, we can release a lot of painful strain to achieve something. Let me put it another way: If we realize that we don't know everything, that we don't control everything, we can engage in conflict without getting wrapped up in it.

By keeping a level head, we are seen as more robust and wiser. You will notice that people respect your opinion more when you act from a place of understanding and good intentions rather than selfishness and blind craving. Starting from a place of compassion and acceptance opens up many doors. By remaining open in this way, there are more paths we can choose to go down.

We can use this gap between us and the conflict to begin questioning our own motivations for how we are acting. We can stop and ask if we are getting upset at this person for something reasonable or simply venting our frustration from a completely different experience.

When we begin to question ourselves in this way, many people are surprised to find that not only are they capable of discerning previously unconscious motives for their actions, but that they have unconscious motives in the first place!

We like to feel in control. We want to think that we have our heads on our shoulders and know what's what. As we get to know ourselves better, we discover that there are many layers to us and that many are usually hidden from sight. Although it may be a little disconcerting to be confronted by your own psychological machinery in this way, it's necessary that we put in the effort to get to know these deeper layers. By becoming familiar with them, we can exert influence over them in a way that would be impossible if we did not understand them.

It's challenging work because sometimes we will see things about ourselves that we would rather not. We may discover that we have tendencies to be anti-social, selfish, manipulative, and many other nasty traits. It isn't until we realize we are jealous and controlling that we can stop being that way. We likely won't succeed entirely since we are who we are. Still, we can recognize when we are acting out aspects of ourselves that we would rather not and take steps to minimize their power in us.

Our relationships become better when *we* become better. The first step in caring for the people around us is to take care of ourselves. Until then, our relationships will be messy, volatile, and confusing. I don't know if you noticed, but a lot of what this section comes down to is practicing acceptance and keeping an open mind. Accepting what life sends our way creates the space necessary to think our actions through. We no longer act in a knee-jerk kind of way.

Before I learned how to do this, I would be confronted with a conflict or some other hiccup in my relationships, and I would act out patterns of behavior I had learned growing up. That meant closing off and running away as best I could. If I didn't like how something was going, that was it; I washed my hands of the whole thing. That wasn't fair to the person trying to relate to me. It wasn't until I started to consciously accept what was happening that I could loosen my grip on the whole thing.

At first, it wasn't easy. I wasn't very good at it, and even when I succeeded in accepting the situation, I was only taking it in my mind, not my actions. With time, I got better at it, and now I feel more capable of dealing with all kinds of people. I'm not as worried that I'll do something stupid and make a fool of myself because I trust myself to behave in a way I feel good about.

There's an old maxim about how we won't get what we want until we give it up. It isn't until we loosen our grip on how conversations go or how people behave, that we get to have people stick around because they *want* to be around us. Just do your best. The rest will follow.

REGULATING our internal state of mind is integral to showing up for people the right way. To that end, I've put together some strategies and exercises for you to use to help you do that.

Breathing

Believe it or not, how we breathe directly impacts our mental health. When we are panicking, our breath becomes short and shallow. If we stop to slow our breathing, we naturally begin to relax. If you ever find yourself in a situation where you are struggling to remain calm, try this breathing exercise. It's called the 4-2-4 breath. It's pretty straightforward. You inhale for four seconds, hold your breath for two seconds, and then exhale for four seconds. Rinse and repeat. This breathing exercise not only gives your mind something to focus on when you feel like your emotions are volatile, but it also brings increased amounts of oxygen into your system, which calms the brain down. It's handy if you recognize your breath becoming shallow and quick.

Grounding

In the digital age, many of us live primarily in our heads. If we're too much in our heads, our reactions to outside events become skewed. For me, I become irritable. Little things that usually wouldn't bother me set me off. That's why it's important to ground ourselves. Grounding has a little bit of a new-age flavor, but it doesn't need to be. We don't necessarily need to go sit under a tree and exchange our energy with it to ground ourselves. However, getting out in nature is a great way to ground ourselves.

It can be as simple as getting back in touch with our senses. So we can look at physical objects around us, as long as it's not a screen. We can touch things and pay attention to the texture. We can pay attention to the smell of where we are. We can eat something and focus on the flavor. By using our bodily senses, we can get out of our heads and back into our bodies. Grounding can sometimes work in the heat of the moment, like focusing on your senses. Still, it is more of a preventative strategy. By keeping yourself grounded, you are more capable of regulating your emotions. Exercise and meditation are my favorite ways of grounding. I'm confident you'll find yours!

ONCE WE GET to know ourselves better, we can identify specific actions or activities we engage in when we feel a particular way. If we tend to avoid people when we are feeling vulnerable or depressed, that's something we can become aware of.

One way to regulate our emotions more effectively is to realize the signs and symptoms of our emotional states. We can then identify when we are feeling a certain way much quicker.

If you play a lot of video games when you're depressed, that's something to notice. If you fidget with your keys when you're anxious, that's something else you can catch. If that emotional state is something you need to remedy, you can then use those signs and actions to help in that process. You do just the opposite. If you avoid people when you feel sad, you should try to find someone to talk to. It probably won't be what you want to do, but by pushing through the discomfort, you can turn the tide and return to feeling healthy and happy.

Journal Prompts

The Stoic's Approach to Emotional Regulation

One of the central themes in this chapter is the Stoic approach to understanding and managing emotions. The misconception that Stoics are cold and emotionless can lead to misunderstandings in relationships. Consider your own interactions and emotions: Have there been times when you may have misunderstood someone's emotional response or lack thereof? Reflect on the idea that just because an emotion isn't outwardly expressed doesn't mean it isn't being felt deeply within. How can understanding and regulating your emotions, without repressing them, lead to more genuine and meaningful relationships in your life? Delve deep into the practice of self-awareness and consider how the Stoic teaching of viewing emotions as messengers can influence your personal relationships and self-growth.

Building Bridges Through Stoic Understanding

Division based on differing beliefs and values is prevalent in our modern society. However, Stoicism promotes understanding, compassion, and empathy, urging us to bridge gaps and foster connections. Reflect on your relationships and interactions with those who hold opposing views or beliefs. How often do you genuinely attempt to understand their perspective? Were there instances where you created barriers instead of bridges? Think about the Stoic approach of accepting what's out of our control, including the beliefs of others. Contemplate the true meaning of being a "force for good" in society. How can you use Stoic teachings to strengthen relationships, even with those you disagree with?

Reflecting on Familial Ties and Personal Growth

Dive deep into your own personal journey with family relationships. Think back to your formative years. What were the key events or incidents that impacted the building blocks of your relationships? Were there any lessons or habits you unconsciously picked up from your family that you wish to change or have already changed?

How did your relationship with your family evolve as you moved into adulthood? Were there any shifts in perceptions, or did you grow more understanding of their flaws? Lastly, how has practicing acceptance, or any other personal development tool, played a role in how you engage with your family now compared to before?

Stoicism and Its Influence on Relationships

Stoicism emphasizes controlling what one can and accepting what one can't. Reflect on the relationships in your life, not just romantic ones but also friendships and your relationship with yourself. How has Stoicism, or understanding and practicing its principles, affected your approach to these relationships? Were there instances where you caught yourself being reactive, and how did stoicism guide you back to calm? When thinking about romantic relationships, how do you balance seeking happiness from your partner and finding joy within yourself? Finally, considering conflicts and disagreements, how has the Stoic perspective of seeing things as 'indifferent' helped you manage your emotional reactions?

SIX
THE LIFE YOU'RE MEANT TO LIVE

"Man conquers the world by conquering himself."

ZENO

I often wonder about what makes living today so unique, how everything is so much different than it used to be. A few hundred years ago, I would have been born into a family with a specific job, like blacksmithing, and I would have grown up and learned how to do that from my parents. I likely would have done that my whole life; the family profession.

Whatever culture I was born into would have predetermined my belief system. Deviation from the belief system of my culture is more severe than it is nowadays, where thinking differently from other people is more or less tolerated.

Most people alive today would find these limitations to be stifling. The lack of freedom to be who you want doesn't exactly entice us. Even still, those people knew who they were, their role in society, and the rules of the game.

Today, everything is up for grabs. Nobody will tell you what to do for work or what you can and can't believe. People will try, but they don't hold any authority, and it's ultimately up to you. This can be liberating, but it can also be a burden. The world is a complex and messy place. In the 21st century, it is up to each individual to decode the mess and make their own way into it.

Some people love the possibilities of such an open-ended system, but many get overwhelmed by it, and we experience an identity crisis. The sheer scale of all possible paths looms large overhead, and we stand in awe and horror at the sight.

Who am I if I can be anything, believe anything? We want something solid to hold onto, but the world is fluid and provides no real answers. For better or worse, it is up to us to discover our life's meaning and purpose.

Luckily we don't need to start entirely from scratch. Stoicism gives us tools to help us better decipher who we are and what we want. It's not like a religion, so it won't give us ready-made answers to some of these questions, but it will help us discover our own solutions.

What is 'Purpose'?

What does it mean to have a purpose in life? It's a seemingly straightforward question but, upon further contemplation, can be a daunting predicament.

When we're young, we usually say something like 'I want to be a doctor' or something to that effect. Some people do find their purpose through their work. It is not unheard of to feel as if your life's purpose is to better society through your vocation. Still, is a purpose the same thing as a profession? Not necessarily. You can find purpose through hobbies, volunteer work, creative pursuits, relationships, you name it.

Knowing our purpose can help us make big life decisions, but it really comes down to meaning-making. When we talk about purpose, we are talking about the aspects of our life that give our lives meaning. We aren't like animals. Human beings are self-aware and driven by narratives. We love stories. Stories help us make sense of the world. Stories tell a series of events that have a sense of progression. The progression from the beginning to middle to end has an arc that helps us understand why the people involved did what they did and how it changed them.

When we talk about purpose, we ask about the story arc in our lives. I was raised in X town, went to Y college, and married Z. Why did I do those things? Was I right to behave in that way? Have I changed over time, and do those changes help me make sense of the chapters in my life?

Sometimes it will feel like you know exactly how your life is going, exactly why you're doing what you're doing, and exactly where you will end up. Five years later, you may feel the exact opposite. You feel everything is a mystery; you don't know who you are or even how you got there.

John Vervaeke, professor of cognitive psychology at the University of Toronto, claims that we are in the middle of a meaning crisis. People are finding it increasingly difficult to find meaning in their lives. He believes that, as we have become more interconnected in a global world, we have started to lose a ready-made narrative for our lives. We are basketball players standing on a tennis court, needing clarification about how to play the game. We need help making ourselves fit into a useful narrative.

Having meaning in our lives is so important. When we feel like life is meaningless, like things happen for no reason or purpose, we risk resorting to unhealthy coping mechanisms.

Stoicism and Meaning

According to Stoicism, the goal for the individual person is to achieve eudaimonia or happiness. If we want to be happy, our lives must have meaning. It's challenging to be truly happy if we feel meaningless.

There are many ways that Stoicism tries to bring meaning to our lives, and they all revolve around the four virtues. In turn, the four virtues revolve around living in agreement with nature. So, in a roundabout way, we bring meaning to our lives when we live in agreement with nature.

Some of that is specific to you, and some are more general. Generally speaking, we live in agreement with nature when we fulfill our duties as human beings. Our purpose is to provide value to society and to our community.

Individually speaking, we live in agreement with nature when we express what we were born to tell. We are meant to take time out of our lives to figure out our passion. Then we bring that particular energy into the world to share with everyone else.

That can look like a lot of different things. Maybe you like helping people. You could work in the medical field or volunteer at a soup kitchen. Perhaps you're creative. In that case, you could teach others how to express their creativity or make something that others will enjoy.

There is an archetype of the wounded healer inside all of us. This is to say that when we confront challenges and obstacles, we become wounded by them in some way. The wounded healer takes the lessons they learned from these experiences and transforms them into something helpful for other people, like medicine.

This archetype is helpful because it helps us make meaning out of suffering. It's easy to get upset about suffering; it's even natural. It's the age-old question of 'Why do bad things happen to good people?' The answer isn't always immediately apparent. Sometimes it feels arbitrary and chaotic, which makes the universe look arbitrary and chaotic.

We can make our suffering as meaningful or as meaningless as we like. Let's say someone loses a loved one and is taken over by grief. It's terrible. They're so angry. Angry at whoever is responsible, angry at themselves and the universe itself. There's a gash across the left side of their chest where this anger pours through. It throbs, and it aches, and it probably always will.

Sometime later, that person could be in two very different places. If they have made their suffering meaningless, the wound has not healed. They don't know how to fix it and may not even understand what's causing them to feel such pain. Their anger has not subsided, and their feeling of meaninglessness has grown quite large.

Another path they could take is to make their suffering meaningful. They embrace their grief. They dive into the wound and understand its purpose. They come out, and the wound has scabbed over. They emerge with something intangible that they can share, like a psychological salve. Because they have had this experience, they can more easily empathize with others.

The wounded healer then takes the healing salve they received from the wound and hands it out to other people. If the wounded healer has helped even just one other person, their suffering has become meaningful. There was a purpose to it. The purpose was to help someone else, and they don't resent their wound anymore because it gave them the knowledge they needed to fulfill that purpose.

Each of us has the potential to be that person and more. There are so many ways to make meaning from our lives. The wounded healer is just one notable path. Our lives are all very different from each other. It's up to us to discover our purpose, like a prospector hunting for gold.

There are many ways to view meaning. As Susan Wolf wrote in her book, *Meaning in Life and Why it Matters*. There is purely subjective meaning-making, where something is meaningful just because someone finds it meaningful.

The problem with this approach is that it suggests any action can be meaningful so long as someone says it is. For instance, if that were true, then alcoholics could potentially be engaged in a highly meaningful life when they drink, so long as they see drinking as fulfilling their purpose. Something about that sounds off, though.

The other way to view meaning is as a hybrid of subjective and objective elements. An activity is meaningful if it is objectively valuable and someone finds value in it.

Helping an elderly neighbor mow their lawn is an objectively valuable thing to do. They would struggle to do it independently, and not doing it would cause them to worry about people judging them for not caring for themselves properly. If you don't want to help, it will probably not give you that much of a sense of purpose, even if it is objectively valuable. On the other hand, if helping your neighbor gives you a feeling of purpose, then what you are doing is meaningful.

An element of discipline and sacrifice here strikes me as relevant. Playing video games non-stop or scrolling through social media endlessly might not be good candidates for meaningful activities because they are self-serving and comfortable. Doing things for ourselves and only ourselves usually won't provide us with this sense of meaning.

For the secularly minded, we could attribute this to human beings evolving as social creatures. We work best when we work together as a community. We have an innate drive to help others, even to our detriment.

For the religious and spiritual among us, we could think of our fundamental need for meaning as our Higher Power's way of pushing us towards a higher level of existence. In a sense, we are engaging with the world in a way that teaches us to value and love others (at least as much as we value ourselves).

The Good, the Bad, and the Indifferent

Part of learning how to put others before ourselves is learning to stop making value judgments. Suppose we must learn to sacrifice some of our comforts to live a meaningful life. In that case, we need to know how to keep ourselves from running away from discomfort.

Stoicism teaches us how to do this by emphasizing the difference between the good, the bad, and the indifferent. Virtue is the only good, according to Stoicism. Those virtues are Wisdom, justice, courage, and moderation. The bad is the opposite of virtue: folly, injustice, cowardice, and indulgence.

Everything else is 'indifferent,' which is to say neutral. On its own, building wealth is neutral. It's not good, and it's not bad; it's indifferent. Dying is indifferent. Losing your job is neither good nor bad. We tend to view whatever is to our detriment as bad, but the moral landscape is actually a lot more nuanced.

If we learn to see the world in this way, we won't have to push through a strong barrier of fear and resistance to what we perceive as detrimental to ourselves. Let's suppose self-sacrifice is an element of living a meaningful life. How much easier will it be to live up to that goal when we have decreased our resistance to 'bad' things happening to us.

If I'm under the impression that it's bad for me to lose money, I will resist that happening. But if I believe that my level of material wealth is neutral, my resistance will be small. Which version will make it easier to donate to a charity?

The same idea can be applied to a variety of situations. The more we resist what we wrongly perceive as bad, the less likely we are to be living up to our highest potential. To live a meaningful life, we must place ourselves in a mindset where self-sacrifice is easier. If we don't, we won't follow through. The task will become too challenging, too demanding.

It won't happen overnight, and it doesn't happen just because you say it out loud. It takes time for this practice to really seep into your life. If you say it's okay to give up your free time on a weekday afternoon to help a friend move, but internally, you are resentful and wish you weren't doing it, you haven't yet embodied the ideas. You're still growing into them.

One day, you may find that sacrifice isn't as hard. You don't mind giving money to charity or volunteering your time. The good that comes from your sacrifice is no longer counterbalanced by your perception of 'bad.' You will only feel the unadulterated good that stems from living a virtuous life.

Finding Your Life Purpose

I wish it were easy to discover your purpose in life, but it's not. It takes concentrated effort and diligent pursuit. Even if you're doing everything 'right,' it may take years to feel like you've found your place in the world. I'm not saying this to discourage you, more to say that my ability to uncover your life's purpose for you may be limited.

Finding your purpose can be fun! It should be fun. You're essentially exploring what you like to do and then going for it. The not-so-fun part is feeling discouraged when circumstances move you away from what you thought your purpose was. Or you may discover that your passion project isn't what you thought it would be. But these are inevitable steps to finding your purpose, so try not to get too down about it.

Your purpose will likely change as you grow up. The purpose your 22-year-old self discovers may be different than the purpose your 36-year-old self finds. It doesn't mean that you have lost your purpose or that you've gone astray. You've just become a different version of yourself, with different desires and drives. Perfectly natural. This continual personal growth keeps life interesting. Because I'm free to evolve, the pressure eases up, and I can enjoy things while they last.

It starts with you asking yourself *about* yourself. To discover our purpose, we must uncover what kind of person we are. We have to get to know ourselves. So that's what we're going to do here. The following are some starter questions that aim to fire up that process of self-discovery. If it helps, grab scrap paper and write down your answers.

What do I enjoy doing?

It's really that simple. Your passions are your inner compass guiding you toward your purpose. Take your time with this one. Whenever you think of something that you really enjoy, add it to the list.

What sparks my interest?

I want to know everything about something when I feel passionate about it. My curiosity is insatiable. Your experience of being interested is unique to you, but my guess is that you know what it feels like when something grabs you.

Think of what brings that feeling out of you. It could be a topic or an activity. If you find dinosaurs unbelievably fascinating, write down dinosaurs. If swimming, medicine, or math does it for you, write it down.

What am I really good at?

Odds are, by the time you've read this book, you've done a few' things.' Were you good at any of them? Did people comment that whatever this thing was that you did was impressive? You can put karaoke here, why not, but try to think of something outside of party tricks and the like.

If money were no obstacle, what would I do?

The funny thing about human beings is that we tend to know the answers. Still, we hide them from ourselves behind twenty different excuses and rationalizations. This is an excellent question for brushing those aside and getting to the point.

Money is no obstacle. You're rich and never need to work again. What would you do with your time if the burdens of life weren't laid on your shoulders? You're totally free. There's a good chance that whatever you say here is exactly what you should be working toward.

What is my life purpose?

No more beating around the bush. No more trying to fool our minds into giving us the answer. First thought, best thought. Write down whatever comes to mind. All correct answers. Just ask the question and, whatever pops into your head, set it on paper. You may be surprised to find that you already know what it is.

Journal Prompts

Navigating Identity and Freedom in Modern Times

In the chapter, the author describes how centuries ago, our destinies were mainly predetermined. We had specific roles to play based on our lineage and community. Today, however, most of the world is characterized by boundless freedom and countless choices. Reflect on your own journey of self-discovery in this era of limitless possibilities. Do you see the freedom to choose your path as a blessing or a curse? Describe moments where this freedom has felt empowering and other times where it has felt overwhelming. How have your cultural upbringing and societal influences shaped your choices, and in what ways have you sought to find a middle ground between embracing unlimited freedom and seeking a sense of identity and belonging?

Crafting Our Personal Narratives

John Vervaeke suggests that we are experiencing a "meaning crisis" as we navigate a world that offers no pre-defined narrative for our lives. Reflect on your own understanding of "purpose." Do you feel you've found a purpose in life, or are you still searching for it? Dive deeper into the stories and narratives that have influenced your journey. What stories (personal, cultural, familial) have shaped your understanding of purpose, and how do these narratives impact your daily decisions and long-term aspirations? Finally, consider the Stoic perspective and its emphasis on living in agreement with nature. How do you reconcile the Stoic teachings with your personal narrative and understanding of purpose?

Navigating Moral Perceptions

Reflect upon a recent event in your life where you found yourself resisting or opposing a certain situation, deeming it 'bad' for yourself. Could that event be seen as merely 'indifferent' in the grand scheme of things? Write down the reasons behind your initial resistance. Next, think about the four core virtues of Stoicism - Wisdom, justice, courage, and moderation. How could embracing these virtues have influenced your perception of the situation? Would your reaction have been different by viewing the event through the lens of Stoicism? Consider how incorporating this philosophy could reshape your future reactions and decisions.

A Personal Quest for Purpose

Reflecting on the provided questions can be a great starting point to uncover your life's purpose. Set aside some quiet time and really delve into each question. For the next week, keep a diary entry dedicated to exploring one of these questions daily. For instance, on Day 1, write extensively about what you truly enjoy doing. Don't limit yourself to just hobbies or pastimes, but think broadly about experiences, interactions, and environments that bring you joy. By Day 7, tackle the question directly: "What is my life purpose?" By dedicating focused time to each question, your answers evolve and become more precise. Compare your Day 7 answer with your initial gut feeling – has the week of reflection changed or sharpened your perspective on your life's purpose?

SEVEN
YOUR END-GOAL: HAPPINESS

"The flourishing life cannot be achieved until we moderate our desires and see how superficial and fleeting they are."

EPICTETUS

With all the talk about self-discipline and virtue, it's easy to lose sight of the real purpose of Stoicism. The stated goal of the whole project is eudaimonia. It's a Greek word often translated as happiness, flourishing, or well-being. Stoicism wants you to be happy. The entire philosophy is built around helping people understand how to live a happy, fulfilling life.

Did you know young adults today are less likely to be happy than twenty years ago? In 1997, 91% of people between 18 and 24 said they were happy. In 2021, that number had dropped a whopping ten points to 81%. This might be a topic for another book, but today's takeaway is that learning how to be happy is needed now more than ever.

Furthermore, happiness is learned. It feels like some people are innately happy; however, a good chunk of us have internal drives which aren't fulfilled. We have needs that aren't being met. If you're reading this book, chances are you're searching for happiness.

First, I need you to know unhappiness is not shameful. It's a tumultuous, angry world, and we're given very little guidance. In a way, we often have to piece together our worldview and best practices for navigating life. This predicament is why strictly adhering to the principles put forth by celebrities, influencers, and self-help gurus is so attractive.

Because we are inundated with "shoulds" and "must haves" by the media, it's easy to feel like you've been hit by the indecisiveness train. So, many ideas come across as exciting and helpful, but upon closer examination, they aren't actually producing the desired result.

Stoicism, however, has been tested over time. This philosophy of life has existed for many centuries and continues to be relevant today. If it was a bunk philosophy, why would anyone even pay attention to it after all these years?

Second, it isn't shallow. This isn't a half-baked idea someone had while they were racking their brain trying to create content to satisfy the algorithm or their audience.

The beauty of Stoicism is that it transcends social media. It existed before technology, algorithms, and hashtags. Its ideas were also developed by different people over the centuries, getting refined and cleaned up until we get what we have today, which is a direct account of how to live your best possible life.

The Obstacles to Happiness

At this point, we should have a solid understanding of how to be a good Stoic. Let's take what we've learned and apply it to the problem the philosophy was built to solve. It might help to reframe the question into something more concrete.

So the question of 'how do we live a good life?' is broken into its components. A good life is a life lived according to our human nature. The obstacles keeping people from achieving the good life can be broken down into two basic camps: 1) making our happiness vulnerable to conditions outside our control and 2) allowing our mental state to be dictated by our emotions.

The first camp is easy to understand but hard to put into practice. To use an extremely not-in-our-control example, let's say we want to win the lottery. All of our hopes and dreams are dependent on that one golden ticket, so to speak. We fantasize about how we'll spend the money and how much happier we'll be when we go on that dream vacation and quit our repetitive, mind-numbing job.

Besides buying the lottery ticket, we have no control over the situation. It's all luck and chance. If we put much of our emotional energy into this happier, wealthier fantasy version of our lives, we set ourselves up for disappointment when we don't win. We are taking our happiness and putting it somewhere else. Instead of creating in-the-moment happiness, we build our happiness on a foundation of "what-ifs."When we discover that we aren't living in the timeline of our fantasies, we are stuck with the timeline of our disappointment. We filter out all of the good and place it outside our real life, in a fantasy.

As humans, we easily fall into the mental trap of using our daydreams to escape our present realities. We do it with our careers, our social life, and our passion projects. We invest our emotional well-being into a metaphorical lottery ticket and then wait to see if we win.

The second camp is probably why the Stoics get a bad rap for emotionlessness. There is a difference between being repressed and being solid, though. If we aren't stable in ourselves, every little breeze will blow us all over the map. Sounds whimsical, but the actual experience isn't.

Thinking about our inner selves gets complicated. Some believe our consciousness comes from our brain, like our brain's software. Others see us as souls living in human bodies. So when we talk about controlling our emotions, where do "we" really stand in this picture?

Think about it: if our consciousness is just in our brain, it's like trying to touch your finger with the same finger. But suppose our consciousness is everywhere, like a universal radio frequency. In that case, finding inner peace means connecting with that more profound level.

I won't claim to have all the answers to these deep questions. But here's the thing: you don't need to know all the technical details to drive a car, right? Similarly, you can learn to manage your emotions without understanding all the mysteries of consciousness.

Achieving Happiness Through Stoicism

There are tools that Stoicism gives us to overcome these obstacles. You're likely familiar with them by now. Still, we'll review them again in this context because some differences are worth noting.

Let's look at the emotional landscape of the world today. We can see that people aren't very good at regulating their emotions. It's not a knock against those people individually. It's just the state of the world we are in. Society has only recently prioritized emotional control. Luckily, it has gifted us the ability to learn if we try.

Our emotional landscape's shortcomings have specific patterns that can help guide us. The rise of social media has trained many of us to think and behave in ways detrimental to our happiness, for example.

In particular, it goes against the wisdom the Stoics shared about value judgments. We are happier when we stop assigning value judgments of good or bad and treat them as neutral. Social media does the opposite. We have 'like' buttons, the algorithm feeds us content it thinks we'll like, and we tend to ostracize perceived bad actions for bad behavior.

On a personal note, I significantly limit my social media use. It makes me depressed, and I find little value in it. I know lots of people who see a lot of value in it. They like the social aspect of it. Their community is stronger because of their ability to share their lives with each other. However, it can't be denied that social media affects how we live, possibly in detrimental ways, if left unchecked.

It's not easy to achieve mental clarity in the digital age. There are so many distractions begging for our attention. Much of our economy is built around 'mining' our attention. Did you know the average person is exposed to somewhere between 6,000 and 10,000 advertisements daily? Advertisers, content creators, influencers, and legacy media, are all fighting tooth and nail for you to look at what they are doing. And they're good at it, too. Everyone's got a job to do, sure. But this professional-grade, high-volume distraction machine makes it difficult to find the mental solidity needed to achieve real happiness.

That being said, getting upset about the state of the world isn't going to help you or anyone else achieve the good life. That's another lesson Stoicism teaches us: amor fati. Love your fate. Accept the life you are given and make of it what you will.

I don't have to embrace things that I don't want in my life. If I'm walking down the street and someone offers me heroin, I'm not Stoically required to accept my fate as a heroin user now. I am free to act in the world and to behave in whatever way fits my values. I am not a passive receptacle, ready to hold whatever the world hands me.

Divine plan or not, the world is going to be what the world is going to be. It's not up to me. I don't have the right to tell the world to conform to my preferences. There is a sense of humility in this, for sure. Understand that your limitations and flaws make you an unsuitable god-king or god-queen.

The popular trend of 'manifesting' wealth, love, and fame can sometimes give the impression that we have complete control over our destinies, possibly overshadowing the value of understanding and accepting life's natural course. This approach often merges the goal of financial success with a spiritual quest for unity and purpose.

While many seek these practices as a path to deeper spirituality and peace of mind, we must remember that increasing desires might sometimes distance us from contentment. Indeed, accepting life as it comes might not always make the most engaging social media content, but its intrinsic value is significant.

Everything you need is already right here. You already have it. People and things will come and go, but there is something within us that never leaves, and it is that thing which is the source of true happiness. It isn't always easy to keep that truth in the forefront of the mind, but once you realize it, it will never truly leave you. If you take the time to get in touch with your inner happiness, you could be working the most stressful job of your life, going through a breakup, and moving to a new place, and you would still have it right there inside you.

All it might take is a little reminder, a description on the back of a book, or a conversation with a friend, and you snap back into it. It may not be the most prominent thing in your mental state, but you will remember everything is okay. You're good.

Living in a healthy mental space like that frees you up. If you believe everything is good, you don't need to hold on to anxiety and worry, you don't need to hold everything you own tight against your chest. You can be open and relaxed, and generous.

A millionaire can still be poor in their mind. Their wealth is not enough. They need more, so they give less and feel threatened by their financial insecurity. At the same time, someone who makes $40,000 a year can feel wealthy. They feel their needs are being met, that life has been good to them, and that whatever happens, they will handle it with courage and compassion.

Wealth exists in the mind. You can have a lot of

money and not be wealthy, or you can have very little money and be quite rich. So long as your basic needs are met, you are free to see the world how you want to. It's all about what you ask of the world.

Happiness Quiz

It's hard to get a good look at yourself. We use other people as a mirror to reflect who we are, but the image we see isn't always clear. It's muddied by our projections and their way of showing up in the world.

So how are we supposed to know our state of mind? Many people use therapy for that. Let's start with something smaller here. I've put together a quiz for you to take to help you discover where you are mentally. Think of it as a tool, not a diagnosis.

Think of the past two months and ask yourself how much each question seems relevant. Grab a sheet of paper and write down the number you pick for the answer: 1, 2, 3, or 4. I'll tell you what to do with it at the end.

I feel heavy and tired.

1. Not at all
2. Sometimes
3. Often
4. All the time!

I think of myself before I think of others.

1. Not at all
2. Sometimes
3. Often
4. All the time!

I don't feel like I am a part of a community.

1. Not at all
2. Sometimes
3. Often
4. All the time!

I have no sense of purpose in my life.

1. Not at all
2. Sometimes
3. Often
4. All the time!

Life feels pointless.

1. Not at all
2. Sometimes
3. Often
4. All the time!

I take myself very seriously.

1. Not at all
2. Sometimes
3. Often
4. All the time!

I don't feel like I have anyone I can turn to.

1. Not at all
2. Sometimes
3. Often
4. All the time!

I rely on substances or entertainment to distract me from my life.

1. Not at all
2. Sometimes
3. Often
4. All the time!

I don't take the time to keep myself healthy.

1. Not at all
2. Sometimes
3. Often
4. All the time!

I don't feel like I have a role to play in the world.

1. Not at all
2. Sometimes
3. Often
4. All the time!

I let relationships slide away instead of maintaining them.

1. Not at all
2. Sometimes
3. Often
4. All the time!

I spend most of my time alone.

1. Not at all
2. Sometimes
3. Often
4. All the time!

I wish something would happen that would make my life better.

1. Not at all
2. Sometimes
3. Often
4. All the time!

I don't spend very much time in nature.

1. Not at all
2. Sometimes
3. Often
4. All the time!

I would rather do something for myself than help someone else.

1. Not at all
2. Sometimes
3. Often
4. All the time!

I spend most of my time staring at a screen.

1. Not at all
2. Sometimes
3. Often
4. All the time!

I feel like I could take a nap.

1. Not at all
2. Sometimes
3. Often
4. All the time!

I don't feel rested when I wake up in the morning.

1. Not at all
2. Sometimes
3. Often
4. All the time!

I don't know what my strengths are.

1. Not at all
2. Sometimes
3. Often
4. All the time!

I don't feel creative or curious.

1. Not at all
2. Sometimes
3. Often
4. All the time!

Now add up all of your answers.
1-20 | You're probably pretty happy!
20-60 | You're sometimes happy.
60-80 | You're likely struggling with your mental well-being.

AS I SAID, the quiz isn't meant to diagnose you. It's more of a tool to help you start thinking about your mental state. If we aren't in the habit of checking in with ourselves, we can often be stuck in a negative mindset without even realizing it.

The brain can rationalize unhealthy ways of being, transforming them into something ordinary. We are highly adaptable creatures. But even though we can adapt to difficult situations doesn't mean that we should resign ourselves to them. We're better than that!

Journal Prompts

Contemplating the Root of Happiness

Reflect on a recent instance when you found your happiness dependent on an external factor or outcome, such as receiving praise, achieving a particular milestone, or acquiring a new possession. Write about the emotions you felt during the anticipation and the aftermath. What impact did achieving or not achieving the desired outcome have on your overall happiness? Considering the Stoic philosophy, how might you approach similar situations in the future to ensure your happiness remains intact and is not contingent on external variables? Think about ways you might shift your focus from external factors to internal contentment and personal growth.

Emotion and Stoic Stability

Recall a recent situation where your emotions seemed to have a hold on your actions or reactions, whether it was an unexpected burst of anger, an overwhelming bout of sadness, or an uncontrollable surge of joy. Describe the situation in detail and your subsequent reactions. Now, using the lens of Stoicism, analyze how recognizing and moderating those emotions might have led to a more stable or constructive outcome. Do you believe that Stoicism advocates for eliminating emotions or understanding and harnessing them?

Social Media's Impact on Perception

In the modern world, the emotional landscape has evolved significantly with the advent of digital technologies, especially social media. Reflect on how social media affects your perception of yourself and the world around you. How do platforms encouraging likes and validations alter your value judgments? Consider the balance between the benefits of social connection these platforms offer and the potential detriments they introduce, such as the perpetual chase for external validation. Does your personal experience with social media align with the author's? In your reflection, detail specific instances or patterns you've noticed in your interactions with these platforms.

Internal Wealth vs. External Affluence

The passage underscores a poignant point: true wealth resides in the mind. A person with immense material assets can feel impoverished, while another with less can feel abundant. Dive deep into your own understanding of wealth and contentment. How do you personally define wealth and success? Do you find yourself associating happiness with materialistic goals or external markers of success? Ponder on experiences or observations from your life where the idea of mental richness over monetary abundance was apparent. How might the Stoic principle of accepting life as it comes and focusing on inner happiness inform your future approach to contentment?

EIGHT

LIFE AS A STOIC: SIMPLE WAYS TO PRACTICE THE PHILOSOPHY EVERY DAY

"Don't seek for everything to happen as you wish it would, but rather wish that everything happens as it actually will—then your life will flow well."

EPICTETUS

As we are nearing the end of our time together, I hope you have started to put the practices of Stoicism to use. If you're still not convinced Stoicism is for you, I encourage you to read the review of the following modern practitioners.

Anna Kendrick, the actress, and singer, told the New York Times that she finds that Stoicism calms her down. Tom Hiddleston, who plays Loki in the Marvel Avengers movies, has tweeted sections of Seneca's On The Shortness of Life. T-Pain, the celebrated R&B artist, has named several of his albums and mixtapes after Stoicism. LL. Cool J, the OG rapper, is a fan of Stoicism, as well. So are prominent businessmen Jack Dorsey, Jonathan Newhouse, and Tim Ferris.

It's a popular philosophy supported by many successful and prominent public figures. One of the reasons Stoicism has seen such a resurgence in the past few years is that people who want to emulate the success of these people have noticed that Stoicism is a common practice among them.

I'm hoping that at this point, you have a general sense of how you can put Stoicism into practice in your life, but knowing something and knowing how to use that something is two different beasts. So we're going to wrap this all together with some ideas of how to take this wisdom and make it actionable.

Daily Stoic Practice

A good morning routine can make or break your day. If we are starting the day off distracted or irritated, the rest of the day is going to follow suit. If we start off from a place of mindfulness and focus, we won't need to struggle as hard to get into that headspace later on.

One way I've found to start my day off on the right foot is limiting my interaction with my phone for the first half hour or so after I wake up. Phones are incredibly useful, but they are also incredibly distracting. There's something about waking up and scrolling through the news or social media or emails when I'm still in bed that puts me in a really weird headspace.

So one way to make sure that you're giving yourself the best chance possible for a great day is to put your phone somewhere out of your reach when you go to sleep. That way, you won't be tempted to lie in bed scrolling first thing in the morning.

On the same note, try to find something that you can do in the morning that does the opposite. Find something that improves your focus and helps keep you relaxed. I've found two ways to do this: exercise and meditation.

These days I prefer exercise. I get active first thing after waking up. It gets my blood flowing, wakes me up, and releases any tension I may have built up the day before. I like doing it first thing in the morning because then I'm not giving myself a chance to make an excuse not to do it. That's what I do first thing, so if I don't do it right, then I'm faltering; there's no "I'll do it later" or anything like that.

Meditation is another great way to start the day. It grounds me in my body and makes the whole world feel so much more open and bright. I love, love, love meditation. There's nothing quite like it. I can't recommend it enough and by doing it in the morning you're getting its lingering effects through the hardest parts of the day.

Another great morning practice is negative visualization. Take a few minutes out of your day and think about all the ways your day can go wrong. We aren't doing this to stress ourselves out or to cause a panic attack, we're doing this to prepare for the worst and to appreciate when those things don't happen.

By practicing negative visualization, we remind ourselves of all the good things in our life. Loved ones we might otherwise take for granted, career opportunities we worked so hard to get but which we tend to forget we achieved, there's plenty of content for this practice.

As a reminder of how negative visualization might work, take something that is going on in your day. Let's say you're in school and you have a test coming up that day. That morning, you can take a minute or two to imagine yourself getting to class and forgetting everything you learned. The test barely makes any sense, and you get a bad grade.

The first part of negative visualization is to prepare for this event. One way to prepare is to study for the test. Make sure that you are as ready as you can be. Another way to prepare is to reassure yourself that even if you did fail the test, your life wouldn't be over. It would suck, but you could buckle down and try harder next time.

The second part of the negative visualization is to appreciate the circumstance. The fact that you are taking this test means that you are in school. You can remind yourself to be grateful for having gotten into this nice college and that you have the money to pay for it or the grades to get a good scholarship.

Another actionable practice is to create Stoic reminders. Write your favorite Stoic quotes on sticky notes and put them around your house or workspace. Join a Stoic email thread. Get Marcus Aurelius' face tattooed on your face. Why not?! Whatever seems right to you, just find ways to remind yourself throughout the day that you are trying to bring Stoicism into your life.

Each of us has a hundred different things pulling us

every which way. We may start our morning out right, but then we get to work, and it all goes out the window. Or our kids need something, or we start to slack off on YouTube. Placing little reminders around you that call you back can help you from accidentally wandering off mentally.

Controlling the Controllable

I've talked a lot about controlling the controllable and accepting what's out of our control, but how do we put that into practice? Well, let's break it down. Controlling the controllable can be boiled down to self-control. You only have control over yourself. If you want to get good at that, you need to practice self-discipline.

One practice you might consider is the Stoic exercise of voluntary discomfort. This involves purposefully placing oneself in slightly uncomfortable situations to build mental resilience. For instance, you could choose to take a colder shower than usual, or you could wear simpler clothing regardless of the weather. It's not about causing harm but rather pushing oneself out of the comfort zone. A friend of mine swears by taking occasional cold showers, claiming that it not only revitalizes him physically but also strengthens his mental resolve.

Lastly, consider refining your consumption habits in

all areas of life. For instance, instead of impulsively buying something you desire, pause and ask yourself whether it's genuinely necessary. Every time you resist an impulsive purchase, you're training your mind to prioritize long-term goals over short-term pleasures. The Stoic perspective isn't about denying oneself joy, but about understanding that true contentment comes from inner harmony and control.

Accepting What's Out of Your Control

The second part of the equation is accepting what's out of our control. This is a major key to living a happier life. The vast majority of the world is not *us*, and it will do whatever it wants, regardless of our wishes. If we want it to behave a certain way and it doesn't, we are prone to getting frustrated or angry.

By learning to accept whatever happens, we are building up our capacity to stomach unfortunate events. We don't need to have our day ruined by every tiny little obstacle. That's a recipe for disaster.

Okay, but how? A lot of it comes down to building muscle memory of non-reactivity. When something bad happens, we tend to react to it immediately. If we want to cut through that reactivity, we need to train our minds to intercept the situation.

Negative visualization can surely help. By preparing for bad things to happen, we aren't as surprised by them, which gives us the opportunity to stay stable. Another really powerful method is to approach life with the assumption of trust.

What I mean by that is this: if we trust that the world will treat us fairly and that whatever obstacles we come across are for our benefit, we don't have as much of a knee-jerk reaction of anger or disappointment. If I spill my coffee and I feel like the world is out to get me, then I'm upset. If I spill my coffee and I feel that the world is on my side, then I brush it off as an accident and move on with my day. Perspective is key.

Stoic Resources

If you're anything like me, now that you've gotten a taste for Stoicism you want more. I've put together a little collection of books, apps, and the like, so you can continue to learn about this life changing philosophy.

Although there are a lot of modern books about Stoicism, it's best to start with the classics. Then you can formulate your own opinions and ideas about Stoicism instead of formulating opinions and ideas about someone else's opinions and ideas.

I'm sure it's no surprise that, *Meditations* by Marcus

Aurelius is an instant recommendation. Although he lived a life very different from us, as an emperor, his notes give great insight into how a healthy mind looks at the world. He offers a lot of insight while also giving a good framework for a role model.

Letters from a Stoic by Seneca is another great piece of Stoicism. The letters were written as advice to his friends, so they're full of practical insights and wisdom. Seneca addresses universal human problems, so even though he is technically addressing someone else, you can still apply it to your own life.

Discourses by Epictetus would be the third must-read Stoic classic. Although he can come across a bit heavy-handed, his insights are spot on, and it's worth pushing through the lecture-style writing to get to the gems of wisdom inside.

If you want something more modern, *The Daily Stoic* is a website run by Ryan Holiday. It's a fantastic resource for articles, exercises, and news revolving around Stoicism in modern life. Holiday has really made a name for himself as one of the prominent modern Stoic figures.

At the time of this writing, the app, "stoic". is a great tool for helping practice emotional resilience. It's like a health tracker for your brain. It offers a place to keep a journal, Stoic quotes, and exercises based on cognitive behavioral therapy to help keep you on track. There's a free plan and a paid plan.

The app, "Stoic Bible" is another great tool to put Stoicism into practice. If you're struggling with keeping up with Stoic practice, this app gives you exercises, access to books and other resources, and guided journaling. It's completely free, although you can pay to remove the ads.

I encourage you to keep learning about yourself and this subject. I also suggest you keep a journal to track your progress as a baby Stoic. If you have a short fuse now, but choose to implement Stoic ideologies or practices, you'll be able to see your patience grow. Take time and enjoy your journey. Remember, there's no perfect way to do this, so identify what works for you and cut out the rest. Happy practicing!

Journal Prompts

Reflecting on Modern Influence

With modern influencers and celebrities practicing Stoicism, how does this affect your perception of the philosophy? Does it encourage you to take it more seriously, or do you believe its wisdom stands independent of popular opinion? Discuss any preconceived notions or biases you may have had towards Stoicism and if they've evolved upon realizing its widespread appeal.

Starting the Day with Stoic Intention

How do you start your day? Reflect on your morning routine and identify any distractions that may throw you off balance. Considering the practices suggested, like exercise, meditation, or negative visualization, which resonates with you the most? How can you implement it in your daily routine? Write about the potential challenges you might face in adhering to this new practice and brainstorm ways to overcome them.

Control and Acceptance

Delve deeper into the idea of controlling what's controllable and accepting what isn't. Recall an event from the past week where you felt a strong emotional reaction. Break it down - was your response due to something within your control or outside of it? How might a Stoic perspective have changed your reaction? Going forward, draft a short mantra or reminder that you can use to keep this Stoic principle at the forefront of your mind.

Resources and Continued Learning

After being introduced to several Stoic resources, both ancient and modern, choose one that piques your interest the most. Why did you select this particular resource? Set a goal for how you plan to engage with it over the next month. This could involve reading several chapters, practicing daily exercises, or simply reflecting on its teachings. By the end of the month, where do you hope this exploration will lead you in your Stoic journey?

CONCLUSION

This is the end of the book. You did it! Thank you so much for taking the time to read this. I hope you get as much out of Stoicism as I know I have. I put this book together as a part of my Stoic practice; to help other people the best way I know how. To that end, thank you for being a part of my journey.

We covered a lot of ground in not a lot of time. There are so many other ways to take your practice to the next level, and I hope I've sparked enough curiosity in you to get you to go seek them out. We all deserve to be happy and to live rich, meaningful lives. Even me and even you.

The world is in a bad way right now. Achieving eudaimonia is not a given. It takes dedication and discipline. It takes conscious intention if we are ever going to get there. Happiness won't stumble across our doorstep one day and stay forever. We have to build something solid and welcoming out of our lives. Only then will happiness find its way to us.

Be patient and learn to truly accept whatever life has to offer. It doesn't only work when things are good. You have to learn how to accept life when it's at its worst if you really want the benefits. That may sound odd but, trust me, it's possible and it's wonderful.

Don't forget to practice what you've learned, either. They're nice ideas, but they don't do anything if you just hang them up on the wall and forget about them. Stoicism is a living, breathing philosophy.

A wise man once said that wisdom is like bread. The recipe may be very old, but every time you use it, you get a warm fresh loaf. I love that so much. He wasn't talking about Stoicism, but it still applies. You can't eat the recipe, you have to bake the bread to really see what all the fuss is about.

We can do it. We can have a happy, fulfilling life, *here and now*, if we just let it be. Everyone is searching for happiness. Everyone wants what Stoicism is offering. These wonderful Stoics have taken the time to figure out how to get there, and they were smart enough to know how to explain it.

I recall a story of an old gardener who tended to his

garden for decades. Every morning, he'd be out there, rain or shine, nurturing his plants, talking to them, and even sometimes singing to them. One day, a young man approached him and remarked, "Why do you spend so much time on these plants? They will grow whether you're here or not." The old gardener smiled and replied, "My dear boy, I don't garden to make the plants grow. I garden to cultivate my soul. It's the daily devotion, the touch of the soil, the scent of the blossoms that bring meaning to my life."

Similarly, Stoicism isn't just about reading and understanding; it's about practicing and living its teachings. Every day, with every challenge and every joy, it's an opportunity to cultivate our souls and embrace the journey toward eudaimonia. Just as the gardener nurtures his plants, we must nurture our understanding and application of Stoicism in our daily lives.

I'm wishing you the best in your pursuit of the good life. I *genuinely* want you to get there.

If you liked the book, and you want to help me reach more people, consider giving the book a review. It helps the book get noticed, which means more people can read it. Thank you for your support, and good luck!

ACKNOWLEDGMENTS

Another huge thanks to Savannah! Big kudos to her for putting up with me and keeping me focused. My books would surely be the scribblings of a madman without her!

JOURNAL PROMPTS

Chapter 1 - It's a Hard-Knock Life

Reflection on Society's State

> *In the chapter, there are references to feelings of societal breakdown, distrust, and polarization. Reflect on your own perceptions of society today. Do you agree with the idea that society is fraying at its seams? Why or why not? Consider your online and offline experiences and interactions and how they shape your views on societal cohesion and unity.*

Navigating Information Overload and Media Perception

The chapter discusses potential distortions in our perceptions due to the influence of media. Reflect on a recent news event or social issue you've come across. How did your primary sources of information present it? In light of the information presented in this chapter, do you believe there's a gap between media representation and reality in certain areas? How do you ensure you're getting an accurate view of events or issues?

Economic Uncertainties and Work Landscape

Economic changes and technological advances like AI pose challenges and opportunities for everyone. The chapter touches on the financial uncertainties younger generations face and the imminent changes in the workforce. How do you feel about the current and future state of the job market, especially in the context of automation? Reflect on whether you believe society and education systems adequately prepare people for these changes. What skills or mindsets do you think will be crucial in the next decade?

Personal Stress and Stoicism

Using the 'Stress Test' presented in the chapter as a guide, delve deeper into your own sources of stress. Identify the three primary stressors in your life and reflect on why they might significantly impact you. Stoicism emphasizes the acceptance of circumstances beyond our control. Which of these stressors can you not change?

Chapter 2 - Stoicism: A Timeless Mindhack

Zeno's Resilience and Personal Setbacks

Zeno experienced a significant setback when his ship sank, resulting in a massive financial loss. Instead of succumbing to despair, he used the experience as a catalyst for personal growth, eventually founding Stoicism*. Reflect on a major setback or challenge you've faced in your own life. How did you initially react? In hindsight, did this event lead to any personal growth or new perspectives? How can you apply* Stoic *principles to future challenges?*

The Illusion of Material Satisfaction

The Stoics*, as highlighted by* Marcus *Aurelius, believed that true happiness does not stem from material possessions. Think about a time you yearned for a material possession, believing it would bring you happiness. Did the joy last? Were you soon looking for the next thing? How can adopting the* Stoic *mindset of "amor fati"* *(love of one's fate) help you find contentment in what you have now?*

The Three Disciplines and Personal Application

The Stoics propose three disciplines for living a good life: the discipline of desire (acceptance), the discipline of action, and the discipline of assent. Which of these disciplines do you feel you most embody daily? Which do you find most challenging? Write about specific instances where you successfully practiced one of these disciplines and moments where you struggled.

Community and Happiness

According to the chapter, achieving true happiness requires engaging with the community and maintaining natural relations. Think about your current relationship with your community. How do you actively contribute to its well-being? Are there areas where you can be more involved or show more love towards fellow human beings? Reflect on your community's role in your happi-

ness and how you can further integrate the Stoic principle of loving engagement for mutual benefit.

Chapter 3 - The Main Mindset: Keep Calm and Carry On

Reflecting on the Four Cardinal Virtues

Consider the Stoic virtues of courage, wisdom, justice, and temperance. How have they appeared in your life? Think about moments when you've embodied these virtues and times you might not have. How can you integrate them more deeply into your daily decisions and behaviors?

The Role of Stoicism in Modern Success

Prominent figures like Warren Buffet, Jeff Bezos, and Elon Musk are said to value Stoicism. Do you believe Stoicism contributes to their achievements? Reflect on your personal definition of success and its alignment with Stoic principles. Would embracing Stoic virtues reshape your measure of success? If so, how?

Embracing Stoic Principles in Daily Life

The chapter introduces ten core Stoic principles, such as living in agreement with nature, amor fati, discerning control, and practicing misfortune, among others. Reflect on a recent challenging situation you encountered. How could these principles have influenced your response or perception of the situation? Identify three principles that could have been particularly relevant, and explore how integrating them has changed your experience.

Stoicism and Personal Well-being

Stoicism promises several benefits, including reduced social anxiety, increased focus, and a deep-seated calm. Think about areas in your life where you feel the need for growth or balance. How might Stoic teachings and mindfulness assist in addressing these areas? Envision a version of your life where you actively apply these principles and describe the changes you anticipate in your mental state and daily actions.

Chapter 4 - How Can Stoicism Help With Stress And Anxiety?

Personal Experiences with Stress and Anxiety

Reflect on your personal experiences with stress and anxiety. Have there been moments in your life where you felt overwhelmed, much like the author's transition to a new job? What were the physical and mental symptoms you experienced? How did these experiences affect your day-to-day life? In your reflection, consider how you've managed or coped with these feelings. Have they been effective? Why or why not? Are there patterns in your life or specific triggers that seem to exacerbate your feelings of stress and anxiety?

Navigating Modern Stress with Stoicism

The author emphasizes the difference between normal stress and anxiety versus chronic or debilitating forms of these feelings. Delve deeper into your understanding of your own stress and anxiety. Are there situations or instances where these reactions are appropriate and beneficial, acting as a protective mechanism? Conversely, are there times when these feelings seem excessive or misaligned with the situation at hand? Consider the role of modern society in this context - do you believe that our current environment exacerbates these feelings? Reflect on how the ancient philosophy of Stoicism might provide tools or perspectives to help you navigate and manage your stress and anxiety in a contemporary setting.

Contemplating Control and Outcomes

Reflect on a recent situation where you felt significant anxiety or stress about an outcome or event. Break down the situation into factors you could control and those you couldn't. How would applying the Stoic principle of "change what you can control and accept what you can't" alter your perspective or emotional reaction to the situation? Dive deep into understanding if your emotional responses were tied more to factors within or outside of your control.

Exploring Negative Visualization

Consider an upcoming event or project that brings anxiety or unease. Practice the Stoic exer-

cise of negative visualization by imagining the worst-case scenarios tied to this event. Be specific in detailing these outcomes. Now, contrast these imagined outcomes with more realistic, probable outcomes. Reflect on how this exercise changes your perception of the event or project. Does envisioning these scenarios make you more prepared, lessen your anxiety, or shift your focus in any way?

Chapter 5 - Stoics are not Hermits: Fostering and Navigating Relationships

The Stoic's Approach to Emotional Regulation

One of the central themes in this chapter is the Stoic approach to understanding and managing emotions. The misconception that Stoics are cold and emotionless can lead to misunderstandings in relationships. Consider your own interactions and emotions: Have there been times when you may have misunderstood someone's emotional response or lack thereof? Reflect on the idea that just because an emotion isn't outwardly expressed doesn't mean it isn't being felt deeply within. How can understanding and regulating your emotions, without repressing them, lead to more genuine and meaningful relationships in your life? Delve deep into the practice of self-awareness and consider how the Stoic teaching of viewing emotions as messengers can influence your personal relationships and self-growth.

Building Bridges Through Stoic Understanding

Division based on differing beliefs and values is prevalent in our modern society. However, Stoicism promotes understanding, compassion, and empathy, urging us to bridge gaps and foster connections. Reflect on your relationships and interactions with those who hold opposing views or beliefs. How often do you genuinely attempt to understand their perspective? Were there instances where you created barriers instead of bridges? Think about the Stoic approach of accepting what's out of our control, including the beliefs of others. Contemplate the true meaning of being a "force for good" in society. How can you use Stoic teachings to strengthen relationships, even with those you disagree with?

Reflecting on Familial Ties and Personal Growth

Dive deep into your own personal journey with family relationships. Think back to your formative years. What were the key events or incidents that impacted the building blocks of your relationships? Were there any lessons or habits you unconsciously picked up from your family that you wish to change or have already changed?

How did your relationship with your family evolve as you moved into adulthood? Were there any shifts in perceptions, or did you grow more understanding of their flaws? Lastly, how has practicing acceptance, or any other personal development tool, played a role in how you engage with your family now compared to before?

Stoicism and Its Influence on Relationships

Stoicism emphasizes controlling what one can and accepting what one can't. Reflect on the relationships in your life, not just romantic ones but also friendships and your relationship with yourself. How has stoicism, or understanding and practicing its principles, affected your approach to these relationships? Were there instances where you caught yourself being reactive, and how did stoicism guide you back to calm? When thinking about romantic relationships, how do you balance seeking happiness from your partner and finding joy within yourself? Finally, considering conflicts and disagreements, how has the

Stoic perspective of seeing things as 'indifferent' helped you manage your emotional reactions?

Chapter 6 - The Life You're Meant to Live

Navigating Identity and Freedom in Modern Times

In the chapter, the author describes how centuries ago, our destinies were mainly predetermined. We had specific roles to play based on our lineage and community. Today, however, most of the world is characterized by boundless freedom and countless choices. Reflect on your own journey of self-discovery in this era of limitless possibilities. Do you see the freedom to choose your path as a blessing or a curse? Describe moments where this freedom has felt empowering and other times where it has felt overwhelming. How have your cultural upbringing and societal influences shaped your choices, and in what ways have you sought to find a middle ground between embracing unlimited freedom and seeking a sense of identity and belonging?

Crafting Our Personal Narratives

John Vervaeke suggests that we are experiencing a "meaning crisis" as we navigate a world that offers no pre-defined narrative for our lives. Reflect on your own understanding of "purpose." Do you feel you've found a purpose in life, or are you still searching for it? Dive deeper into the stories and narratives that have influenced your journey. What stories (personal, cultural, familial) have shaped your understanding of purpose, and how do these narratives impact your daily decisions and long-term aspirations? Finally, consider the Stoic perspective and its emphasis on living in agreement with nature. How do you reconcile the Stoic teachings with your personal narrative and understanding of purpose?

Navigating Moral Perceptions

Reflect upon a recent event in your life where you found yourself resisting or opposing a certain situation, deeming it 'bad' for yourself. Could that event be seen as merely 'indifferent' in the grand scheme of things? Write down the reasons behind your initial resistance. Next, think about the four core virtues of Stoicism - Wisdom, justice, courage, and moderation. How could embracing these virtues have influenced your perception of the situation? Would your reaction have been different by viewing the event through the lens of Stoicism? Consider how incorporating this philosophy could reshape your future reactions and decisions.

A Personal Quest for Purpose

Reflecting on the provided questions can be a great starting point to uncover your life's purpose. Set aside some quiet time and really delve into each question. For the next week, keep a diary entry dedicated to exploring one of these questions daily. For instance, on Day 1, write extensively about what you truly enjoy doing. Don't limit yourself to just hobbies or pastimes, but think broadly about experiences, interactions, and environments that bring you joy. By Day 7, tackle the question directly: "What is my life purpose?" By dedicating focused time to each question, your answers evolve and become more precise. Compare your Day 7 answer with your initial gut feeling – has the week of reflection changed or sharpened your perspective on your life's purpose?

Chapter 7 - Your End-Goal: Happiness

Contemplating the Root of Happiness

Reflect on a recent instance when you found your happiness dependent on an external factor or outcome, such as receiving praise, achieving a particular milestone, or acquiring a new possession. Write about the emotions you felt during the anticipation and the aftermath. What impact did achieving or not achieving the desired outcome have on your overall happiness? Considering the Stoic philosophy, how might you approach similar situations in the future to ensure your happiness remains intact and is not contingent on external variables? Think about ways you might shift your focus from external factors to internal contentment and personal growth.

Emotion and Stoic Stability

Recall a recent situation where your emotions seemed to have a hold on your actions or reactions, whether it was an unexpected burst of anger, an overwhelming bout of sadness, or an uncontrollable surge of joy. Describe the situation in detail and your subsequent reactions. Now, using the lens of Stoicism, analyze how recognizing and moderating those emotions might have led to a more stable or constructive outcome. Do you believe that Stoicism advocates for eliminating emotions or understanding and harnessing them?

Social Media's Impact on Perception

In the modern world, the emotional landscape has evolved significantly with the advent of digital technologies, especially social media. Reflect on how social media affects your perception of yourself and the world around you. How do platforms encouraging likes and validations alter your value judgments? Consider the balance between the benefits of social connection these platforms offer and the potential detriments they introduce, such as the perpetual chase for external validation. Does your personal experience with social media align with the author's? In your reflection, detail specific instances or patterns you've noticed in your interactions with these platforms.

Internal Wealth vs. External Affluence

The passage underscores a poignant point: true wealth resides in the mind. A person with immense material assets can feel impoverished, while another with less can feel abundant. Dive deep into your own understanding of wealth and contentment. How do you personally define wealth and success? Do you find yourself associating happiness with materialistic goals or external markers of success? Ponder on experiences or observations from your life where the idea of mental richness over monetary abundance was apparent. How might the Stoic principle of accepting life as it comes and focusing on inner happiness inform your future approach to contentment?

Chapter 8 - Life as a Stoic: Simple Ways to Practice the Philosophy Every Day

Reflecting on Modern Influence

With modern influencers and celebrities practicing Stoicism, how does this affect your perception of the philosophy? Does it encourage you to take it more seriously, or do you believe its wisdom stands independent of popular opinion? Discuss any preconceived notions or biases you may have had towards Stoicism and if they've evolved upon realizing its widespread appeal.

Starting the Day with Stoic Intention

How do you start your day? Reflect on your morning routine and identify any distractions that may throw you off balance. Considering the practices suggested, like exercise, meditation, or negative visualization, which resonates with you the most? How can you implement it in your daily routine? Write about the potential challenges you might face in adhering to this new practice and brainstorm ways to overcome them.

Control and Acceptance

Delve deeper into the idea of controlling what's controllable and accepting what isn't. Recall an event from the past week where you felt a strong emotional reaction. Break it down - was your response due to something within your control or outside of it? How might a Stoic perspective have changed your reaction? Going forward, draft a short mantra or reminder that you can use to keep this Stoic principle at the forefront of your mind.

Resources and Continued Learning

After being introduced to several Stoic resources, both ancient and modern, choose one that piques your interest the most. Why did you select this particular resource? Set a goal for how you plan to engage with it over the next month. This could involve reading several chapters, practicing daily exercises, or simply reflecting on its teachings. By the end of the month, where do you hope this exploration will lead you in your Stoic journey?

ABOUT THE AUTHOR

Jordan T. Beckett is a dedicated author who has made it his mission to empower and uplift all through his inspiring books. As an avid researcher in psychology and personal development, Jordan is deeply committed to helping his readers navigate the challenges of adulthood with confidence.

Having experienced his fair share of ups and downs, Jordan brings a relatable and empathetic approach to his writing. He understands the struggles and pressures that people face in today's fast-paced world and is determined to provide them with the tools and strategies they need to overcome obstacles and thrive.

Through his books, Jordan combines practical advice, insightful anecdotes, and actionable steps to guide readers toward personal growth and success. He covers many topics, including self-esteem, goal setting, relationships, and mental well-being, offering invaluable wisdom that resonates with his audience.

Jordan's writing style is engaging and accessible,

making his books a joy to read for both seasoned self-help enthusiasts and those new to the genre. His genuine passion for peoples' well-being shines through every page, motivating and inspiring readers to take control of their lives and make positive changes.

When he's not writing, Jordan enjoys making music, spending time in nature, and connecting with his readers online. He believes in the power of human connection and strives to create a supportive community where everyone can thrive and find solace in their shared experiences.

Jordan T. Beckett empowers people to become their best versions through his heartfelt approach. His books are essential for anyone seeking guidance, motivation, and a roadmap to success in life's exciting and sometimes challenging journey.

Scan to explore more of his works!

BIBLIOGRAPHY

———. "What We Know About Gen Z So Far | Pew Research Center." Pew Research Center's Social & Demographic Trends Project, May 22, 2023. https://www.pewresearch.org/social-trends/2020/05/14/on-the-cusp-of-adulthood-and-facing-an-uncertain-future-what-we-know-about-gen-z-so-far-2/.

Pew Research Center. "52% of Young Adults in US Are Living with Their Parents amid COVID-19 | Pew Research Center," September 9, 2020. https://www.pewresearch.org/fact-tank/2020/09/04/a-majority-of-young-adults-in-the-u-s-live-with-their-parents-for-the-first-time-since-the-great-depression/.

"Study: Parents Are the Biggest Financial Influence for 1 in 3 Young Adults," n.d. https://www.thezebra.com/resources/research/financial-independence-report/#key-finding-4.

Mitchell, Travis. "Most Americans Say Parents Do Too Much for Their Young Adult Children | Pew Research Center." Pew Research Center's Social & Demographic Trends Project, July 10, 2023. https://www.pewresearch.org/social-trends/2019/10/23/majority-of-americans-say-parents-are-doing-too-much-for-their-young-adult-children/.

Deloitte. "Who We Are," June 5, 2023. https://www2.deloitte.com/global/en/pages/about-deloitte/articles/millennialsurvey.html?id=us:2el:3dp:wsjspon:awa:WSJCMO:2021:WSJFY21.

WSJ. "Top Stress Factors for Millennials, Gen ZS," August 23, 2021. https://deloitte.wsj.com/articles/top-stress-factors-for-millennials-gen-zs-01629738257.

Rainosek, Callie. "Gen Z and Millennials Are Stressed 'Basically at All Times.'" *Salud America*, November 9, 2022. https://salud-america.org/gen-z-and-millennials-are-stressed-basically-at-all-times/.

Allan. “A Glossary Of Common Stoicism Terms.” *What Is Stoicism?*, July 25, 2022. https://whatisstoicism.com/Stoicism-definition/a-glossary-of-common-Stoicism-terms/.

Mind, Warrior of The. “Stoic Terminology.” WARRIOR OF THE MIND, n.d. https://thewarriorofthemind.com/pages/Stoic-terminology.

Borge, Jonathan, and Elena Nicolaou. “Here’s What All of Those Popular Slang Words Really Mean.” *Oprah Daily*, April 27, 2023. https://www.oprahdaily.com/entertainment/g23603568/slang-words-meaning/.

Liles, Maryn. “50 Gen Z Slang Words You Need To Know To Keep From Becoming ‘Cheugy.’” *Parade: Entertainment, Recipes, Health, Life, Holidays*, June 2, 2023. https://parade.com/1293898/marynliles/gen-z-slang-words/.

Mbacp, Michael Swift Integrative Psychotherapist | MSc. “How Stoicism Changed My Life… and Can Change Yours Too.” *Counselling Directory*, August 8, 2021. https://www.counselling-directory.org.uk/memberarticles/how-Stoicism-changed-my-life-and-can-change-yours-too#:~:text=The%20Stoics%20recognised%20that%20there,way%20we%20respond%20to%20them.

Holiday, Ryan. “The Definitive List of Stoicism in History & Pop Culture.” *Daily Stoic*, November 25, 2017. https://dailystoic.com/stoicism-pop-culture/.

Knight, Ivy. “Stoic Philosophy Goes Hollywood.” *The New Yorker*, January 24, 2022. https://www.newyorker.com/magazine/2022/01/31/stoic-philosophy-goes-hollywood.

Cox, Brian, and Brian Cox. “Famous Stoics in History and Pop Culture.” Living by Example, September 5, 2022. https://www.livingbyexample.org/famous-stoics-in-history-and-pop-culture/.

West, Steven. "Stoics in the Modern World: 5 Famous Stoics Who Might Surprise You." *Critical Thinking Secrets*, June 29, 2023. https://criticalthinkingsecrets.com/stoics-in-the-modern-world/.

University of California San Francisco. "48% of Young Adults Struggled with Mental Health in Mid-2021 | UC San Francisco." *48% of Young Adults Struggled With Mental Health in Mid-2021 | UC San Francisco*, April 9, 2022. https://www.ucsf.edu/news/2022/04/422611/48-young-adults-struggled-mental-health-mid-2021.

Rm-Admin. "Understanding the Challenges Young People Face in 2021 and Beyond." *Round Midnight*, January 19, 2021. https://www.roundmidnight.org.uk/understanding-the-challenges-young-people-face-in-2021-and-beyond/.

Book Therapy. "Who Am I? The Identity Crisis Faced by Millennials Today," November 17, 2019. https://www.booktherapy.io/blogs/news/who-am-i-the-identity-crisis-faced-by-millennials-today.

Raval, Nikhil. "Is the Gen Z Generation Facing an Identity Crisis?" *Www.Linkedin.Com*, n.d. https://www.linkedin.com/pulse/gen-z-generation-facing-identity-crisis-nikhil-raval.

"'Milestone Anxiety' on the Rise among Millennials and Gen Z | Relate," n.d. https://www.relate.org.uk/get-help/milestone-anxiety-rise-among-millennials-and-gen-z.

Author, iGrad. "The Top 5 Financial Issues Millennials Face Today." *The Well* (blog), November 14, 2022. https://www.enrich.org/blog/the-top-5-financial-issues-millennials-face-today.

Weil, Dan. "Money Worries Hit Millennials and Gen-Z Hard." *TheStreet*, October 21, 2022. https://www.thestreet.com/personal-finance/money-worries-hit-millenials-and-gen-z-hard.

Cohen, Mikaela. "The Pandemic 'Quickly Eroded Savings' for Gen Z, Millennials: Study." *CNBC*, February 12, 2022. https://www.cnbc.com/2022/02/12/the-pandemic-quickly-eroded-savings-for-gen-z-millennials-study.html.

www.cbc.ca. "Generation 'Fear': How Bad News Has Created an Anxious Generation," n.d. https://www.cbc.ca/documentarychannel/features/generation-fear-how-bad-news-has-created-an-anxious-generation.

Kohrman, Miles. "Young People Fear Gun Violence, But Also Think Guns May Keep Them Safe." *The Trace*, September 28, 2022. https://www.thetrace.org/2022/09/youth-study-mass-shooting-mental-health/.

Nadeem, Reem. "Gen Z, Millennials Stand out for Climate Change Activism, Social Media Engagement with Issue | Pew Research Center." Pew Research Center Science & Society, May 22, 2023. https://www.pewresearch.org/science/2021/05/26/gen-z-millennials-stand-out-for-climate-change-activism-social-media-engagement-with-issue/.

Yale E360. "For Gen Z, Climate Change Is a Heavy Emotional Burden," n.d. https://e360.yale.edu/features/for-gen-z-climate-change-is-a-heavy-emotional-burden.

Bagenstose, Kyle, and Usa Today. "The Kids Are All Fight: How Millennials and Gen Z Are Driving Change on Climate." *Phys*, August 23, 2022. https://phys.org/news/2022-08-kids-millennials-gen-climate.html.

Rios, Preston. "Social Media Caused Gen. Z and Millennials to Be out of Touch with Reality." North Texas Daily, September 28, 2020. https://www.ntdaily.com/social-media-caused-gen-z-and-millennials-to-be-out-of-touch-with-reality/.

"48% of Gen Z Say Social Media Makes Them Feel Anxious, Sad or Depressed 58% Are 'Seeking Relief' from Social Media," n.d. https://www.businesswire.com/news/home/20191024005627/en/48-of-Gen-Z-Say-Social-Media-Makes-Them-Feel-Anxious-Sad-or-Depressed-58-Are-%E2%80%9CSeeking-Relief%E2%80%9D-from-Social-Media.

"Bloomberg - Are You a Robot?," September 6, 2022.

https://www.bloomberg.com/news/articles/2022-09-06/pressure-to-reach-life-milestones-affecting-younger-generations-more-research#xj4y7vzkg.

"'Milestone Anxiety' on the Rise among Millennials and Gen Z | Relate," n.d. https://www.relate.org.uk/get-help/milestone-anxiety-rise-among-millennials-and-gen-z.

Larson, Hannah. "Gen Z Battles Negative Body Image amid Unrealistic Beauty Standards." *The Chimes*, October 20, 2022. https://chimesnewspaper.com/52142/showcase/gen-z-battles-negative-body-image-amid-unrealistic-beauty-standards/.

Relative Insight. "Let's Talk about Bodies: How Millennials and Gen Z View Theirs - Relative Insight," October 19, 2021. https://relativeinsight.com/case-studies/how-millennials-and-gen-z-view-body-image-text-analysis-social-data/.

Zahair, Akeela. "Millennials Have the Least Body Confidence in 2020 - GHP News." GHP News, January 12, 2021. https://www.ghp-news.com/millennials-have-the-least-body-confidence-in-2020/.

Jordan. "Millennials and Gen Z-Ers Are Uncertain About the Future." *HR ASIA*, May 29, 2019. https://hr.asia/featured-news/millennials-and-gen-z-ers-are-uncertain-about-the-future/.

People Matters. "People Matters - Interstitial Site — People Matters," n.d. https://www.peoplematters.in/article/strategic-hr/engaging-millennials-and-gen-z-in-the-times-of-uncertainty-30419.

Jonathan Lee Recruitment. "Millennials: Riding The Wave Of Uncertainty," n.d. https://www.jonlee.co.uk/blog/2019/01/millennials-the-generation-riding-the-wave-of-uncertainty?source=google.com.

YPulse. "Which Social Causes & Issues Are Gen Z and Millennials Most Passionate About in 2023? - YPulse," February 23, 2023. https://www.ypulse.com/article/2023/02/23/which-social-causes-issues-are-gen-z-and-millennials-most-passionate-about-in-2023/.

Contributor, Deloitte. "For Millennials And Gen Zs, Social Issues Are Top Of Mind—Here's How Organizations Can Drive Meaningful Change." *Forbes*, July 22, 2021. https://www.forbes.-com/sites/deloitte/2021/07/22/for-millennials-and-gen-zs-social-issues-are-top-of-mind-heres-how-organizations-can-drive-meaningful-change/.

Deloitte Montenegro. "In Its 10th Year, the Deloitte Global Millennial and Gen Z Survey Reveals Two Generations Pushing for Social Change and Accountability," n.d. https://www2.deloitte.-com/me/en/pages/about-deloitte/articles/in-its-10th-year-the-deloitte-global-millennial-and-gen-z-survey-reveals-two-generations-pushing-for-social-change-and-accountability.html.

Deloitte. "Millennials, Gen Z and Mental Health," January 23, 2023. https://www.deloitte.com/global/en/about/people/social-responsibility/millennials-gen-z-and-mental-health.html.

Bethune, Sophie. "Gen Z More Likely to Report Mental Health Concerns." *Https://Www.Apa.Org*, n.d. https://www.a-pa.org/monitor/2019/01/gen-z.

Lucchesi, Emilie Le Beau. "Mental Health Problems Increase In Millennials and Gen Z, New Study Reports." *Discover Magazine*, June 28, 2022. https://www.discovermagazine.-com/mind/mental-health-problems-increase-in-millennial-and-gen-z-new-study-reports.

Chettiarcounselling. "5 Common Issues That Young Adults of Today Face." *Blog | Chettiar Counselling and Associates*, June 29, 2023. https://chettiarcounselling.ca/blog/issues-young-adults-today-face/.

D'Amico, Pat. "Common Challenges Young Adults Face Today." *Paradigm Treatment Mental Health Treatment For Teens and Young Adults* (blog), July 19, 2023. https://paradigmtreatment.-com/challenges-young-adults-facing-today/.

———. "Understanding the Challenges Young People Face in 2021 and Beyond." *Round Midnight*, January 19, 2021.

https://www.roundmidnight.org.uk/understanding-the-challenges-young-people-face-in-2021-and-beyond/.

https://www.ypulse.com/article/2022/06/14/the-biggest-problem-gen-z-and-millennials-say-theyre-facing-in-2022/

Li, Diane. "Being 20-Something in 2023 - Diane Li - Medium." *Medium*, March 30, 2023. https://medium.com/@dianee.li/being-20-something-in-2023-54b00859a2d3.

Burton, Andalis. "Why Gen Z Is the Most Stressed Generation in the Workplace (2023)." *Medium*, August 3, 2023. https://medium.com/@andalis/why-gen-z-is-the-most-stressed-generation-in-the-workplace-2023-90e9a6385afd.

Kumar, R Pavan. "Here Are the Observations I Made about Gen Z. - R Pavan Kumar - Medium." *Medium*, January 16, 2023. https://medium.com/@pavankumar10998/here-are-the-observations-i-made-about-gen-z-5a63c55ca4d9.

Greater Good. "Stress and Anxiety Quiz," n.d. https://greatergood.berkeley.edu/quizzes/take_quiz/stress_and_anxiety.

Mandriota, Morgan. "Stress Level Test: How Stressed Are You?" Psych Central, May 18, 2022. https://psychcentral.com/quizzes/stress-test#take-the-quiz.

Be Mindful. "Test Your Stress | Be Mindful," August 12, 2023. https://www.bemindfulonline.com/test-your-stress.

Holiday, Ryan. "Dealing With Stress: 12 Proven Strategies For Stress Relief From Stoicism." *Daily Stoic*, February 16, 2021. https://dailystoic.com/stress-relief/#what-did-the-stoics-think-about-stress.

———. "These 5 Stoic Strategies Will Help You Slay Your Stress." *Medium*, January 7, 2022. https://forge.medium.com/these-5-stoic-strategies-will-help-you-slay-your-stress-86f6e38fa71b.

P, Lorna. "How to Be a Stoic & Manage Stress." *Utopia*, December 22, 2022. https://utopia.org/guide/how-to-be-a-stoic-manage-stress/.

Rad, Dave. "Stoicism 101: An Introduction to Stoicism, Stoic Philosophy and the Stoics." *Holstee*, January 1, 2018. https://www.holstee.com/blogs/mindful-matter/stoicism-101-everything-you-wanted-to-know-about-stoicism-stoic-philosophy-and-the-stoics.

Saunders, Jason Lewis. "Stoicism | Definition, History, & Influence." Encyclopedia Britannica, August 8, 2023. https://www.britannica.com/topic/Stoicism.

LotusBuddhas. "What Is Stoicism? Definition, History and Practices." *LotusBuddhas*, June 9, 2023. https://lotusbuddhas.-com/what-is-stoicism.html#definition-of-stoicism.

———. "What Is Stoicism? A Definition & 9 Stoic Exercises To Get You Started." *Daily Stoic*, March 7, 2022. https://dailystoic.-com/what-is-stoicism-a-definition-3-stoic-exercises-to-get-you-started/#what-is-stoicism.

Stoic Reflections. "An Introduction to Stoicism | Stoic Reflections," July 17, 2023. https://stoicreflections.com/blogs/articles/an-introduction-to-stoicism.

Stoic Journey. "A Brief History of Stoicism," November 9, 2019. https://stoicjourney.org/2016/07/28/a-brief-history-of-stoicism/.

———. "What Is Stoicism? Definition, History and Practices." *LotusBuddhas*, June 9, 2023. https://lotusbuddhas.com/what-is-stoicism.html#definition-of-stoicism.

Salzgeber, Jonas. "What Is Stoicism? A Definition & 10 Stoic Key Principles." NJlifehacks, April 12, 2019. https://www.njlifehacks.com/what-is-stoicism-overview-definition-10-stoic-principles/#tab-con-18.

Lesso, Rosie. "What Are the Origins of Stoicism?" *TheCollector*, April 28, 2023. https://www.thecollector.com/what-are-the-origins-of-stoicism-history/.

Drew, Simon. "A Brief History of Stoicism." *Poet | Musician | Philosophical Mentor | Creativity Mentor*, September 2, 2020. https://www.simonjedrew.com/a-brief-history-of-stoicism/.

———. "What Are the Origins of Stoicism?" *TheCollector*, April 28,

2023. https://www.thecollector.com/what-are-the-origins-of-stoicism-history/.

Bat, Thinking. "Story of Stoicism and the Birth of Cognitive Behavioral Therapy." *The Thinking Bat Newsletter*, February 1, 2022. https://thinkingbat.substack.com/p/stoicism-the-father-of-cbt.

Awake. "The Ancient History of Cognitive Behavioural Therapy - Awake ®." Awake ®, May 26, 2021. https://awakespace.-co/blog/the-ancient-history-of-cognitive-behavioural-therapy/.

Donald J. Robertson. "Introduction to Stoicism: The Three Disciplines," August 25, 2022. https://donaldrobertson.-name/2013/02/20/introduction-to-stoicism-the-three-disciplines/.

———. "What Are The Three Stoic Disciplines?" *What Is Stoicism?*, May 16, 2022. https://whatisstoicism.com/stoicism-definition/what-are-the-three-stoic-disciplines/.

Street, Farnam. "The Three Disciplines of Stoicism: Life Lessons from a Roman Emperor." *Farnam Street*, March 1, 2020. https://fs.blog/important-life-lessons-courtesy-of-a-roman-emperor/.

Vivo Life EU. "How Stoicism Changed My Life," August 7, 2020. https://eu.vivolife.com/blogs/news/how-stoicism-changed-my-life.

Economy, Peter. "Jeff Bezos, Elon Musk, Bill Gates, and Warren Buffett All Use This Ancient Philosophy to Build Wealth." *Inc.Com*, February 6, 2020. https://www.inc.com/peter-economy/bezos-musk-gates-and-buffett-use-this-ancient-phil.html.

Contributor. "7 Ways Billionaires like Warren Buffett and Bill Gates Demonstrate the Ancient Philosophy of Marcus Aurelius." *Business Insider*, June 8, 2017. https://www.businessinsider.-com/stoic-philosophy-exercises-2017-6.

Weaver, Tobias. "How To Get Started With Stoicism." *Orion Philosophy*, April 15, 2023. https://www.orionphilosophy.com/stoic-blog/stoicism-how-to-get-started.

———. "What Is Stoicism? Definition, History and Practices." *LotusBuddhas*, June 9, 2023. https://lotusbuddhas.com/what-is-stoicism.html#definition-of-stoicism.

PsyD, Christopher L. Heffner, PhD. "Stoicism, Virtue, and Mental Health - AllPsych." *AllPsych - The Virtual Psychology Classroom* (blog), July 5, 2022. https://allpsych.com/stoicism-virtue-and-mental-health/.

Lake, Tim. "An In-Depth Understanding on the Four Virtues of Stoicism." *TheCollector*, March 20, 2023. https://www.thecollector.com/four-cardinal-virtues-stoicism/.

MacRae, Brechen. "How To Practice The 4 Stoic Virtues." *The Mindful Stoic*, March 25, 2023. https://mindfulstoic.net/practicality-and-the-4-stoic-virtues/.

Merton, Sophia, and Sophia Merton. "Stoic Virtues: A Short Introduction to the 4 Stoic Virtues." *Stoic Quotes - The Best Stoic Quotes on Life and Philosophy.* (blog), July 20, 2023. https://stoicquotes.com/stoic-virtues/#how_to_practice_the_four_stoic_virtues.

———. "What Is Stoicism? A Definition & 10 Stoic Key Principles." NJlifehacks, April 12, 2019. https://www.njlifehacks.com/what-is-stoicism-overview-definition-10-stoic-principles/#tab-con-18.

Dubey, Damayanti. "Stoicism: Definition & 10 Principles of Stoicism For Better Life | Evolve US." *Evolve* (blog), February 2, 2022. https://evolveinc.io/self-improvement/10-stoic-principles/#10_Stoic_Principles.

Loper, Chris. "10 Essential Principles and Practices of Stoicism." *Becoming Better*, September 19, 2022. https://becomingbetter.org/10-essential-principles-and-practices-of-stoicism/.

Gill, N.S. "Stoics and Moral Philosophy - The 8 Principles of Stoicism." *ThoughtCo*, October 25, 2019. https://www.thoughtco.com/stoics-and-moral-philosophy-4068536.

Jay. "What Are the 8 Principles of Stoicism? - Mind by Design."

Mind by Design, July 29, 2021. https://www.mindbydesign.io/8-principles-of-stoicism/.

Underwood, Brent. "7 Benefits of Adopting a Stoic Practice in 2020." *Daily Stoic*, January 13, 2020. https://dailystoic.com/benefits-stoicism/.

Nasr, Simon. "Top Five Benefits of Stoic Philosophy: From Presence to Self-Actualization." *The Wise Mind*, August 17, 2020. https://thewisemind.net/top-five-benefits-of-stoic-philosophy-from-presence-to-self-actualization/.

Merton, Sophia, and Sophia Merton. "How to Be a Stoic: A Beginner's Guide to Practicing Stoicism." *Stoic Quotes - The Best Stoic Quotes on Life and Philosophy.* (blog), July 20, 2023. https://stoicquotes.com/how-to-be-a-stoic/#what_are_the_benefits_of_adopting_a_stoic_mindset.

Vivo Life EU. "How Stoicism Changed My Life," August 7, 2020. https://eu.vivolife.com/blogs/news/how-stoicism-changed-my-life.

Harte, Enda. "The Cardinal Virtues of Stoicism - Stoicism — Philosophy as a Way of Life - Medium." *Medium*, March 9, 2023. https://medium.com/stoicism-philosophy-as-a-way-of-life/the-cardinal-virtues-of-stoicism-41ac08314936.

Eloy. "Reddit - Dive into Anything," n.d. https://www.reddit.com/r/Stoicism/comments/7hp6xa/a_first_attempt_to_put_virtue_graphically_would/.

Maloma, Tiisetso. "14 STOICISM QUOTES THAT HELP HEAL ANXIETY - Defuse Anxiety - Medium." *Medium*, July 15, 2022. https://medium.com/defuse-anxiety/14-quotes-stoicism-healing-for-the-anxious-entrepreneur-38ca8827511d#.

Northwestern. "'Stress in America' Survey Reveals Mental Health of Young Adults as Most at-Risk," n.d. https://news.northwestern.edu/stories/2020/10/stress-in-america-2020-survey-reveals-mental-health-of-young-adults-as-most-at-risk/.

Mental Health Foundation. "60% of Young People Unable to Cope

Due to Pressure to Succeed," n.d. https://www.mental-health.org.uk/about-us/news/60-young-people-unable-cope-due-pressure-succeed.

"Stress," June 17, 2022. https://www.who.int/news-room/questions-and-answers/item/stress#:~:text=What%20is%20stress%3F,experiences%20stress%20to%20some%20degree.

Scott, Elizabeth, PhD. "What Is Stress?" *Verywell Mind*, November 7, 2022. https://www.verywellmind.com/stress-and-health-3145086#toc-signs-of-stress.

The Healthline Editorial Team. "Everything You Need to Know about Stress." Healthline, February 25, 2020. https://www.healthline.com/health/stress.

National Library of Medicine. "Anxiety," n.d. https://medlineplus.gov/anxiety.html#.

Cirino, Erica. "Everything You Need to Know about Anxiety." Healthline, September 17, 2018. https://www.healthline.com/health/anxiety-symptoms.

Bence, Sarah. "Anxiety Symptoms." *Verywell Health*, June 16, 2022. https://www.verywellhealth.com/anxiety-symptoms-5086955.

———. "Everything You Need to Know about Stress." Healthline, February 25, 2020. https://www.healthline.com/health/stress#anxiety.

Michaelepstein. "What Is the Correlation Between Anxiety and Stress?" *Family Psychiatry & Therapy*, February 28, 2020. https://familypsychnj.com/2017/07/correlation-anxiety-stress/.

Tate, Katherine, and Katherine Tate. "5 Ways Stoicism Can Help Ease Anxiety." *WellBeing Magazine*, June 4, 2019. https://www.wellbeing.com.au/mind-spirit/mind/stoicism.html.

———. "Dealing With Stress: 12 Proven Strategies For Stress Relief From Stoicism." *Daily Stoic*, February 16, 2021. https://dailystoic.com/stress-relief/.

———. "These 5 Stoic Strategies Will Help You Slay Your Stress."

Medium, January 7, 2022. https://forge.medium.com/these-5-stoic-strategies-will-help-you-slay-your-stress-86f6e38fa71b.

Edblad, Patrik. "How to Relieve Stress & Anxiety." *Patrik Edblad*, August 11, 2020. https://patrikedblad.com/stoicism/relieve-stress-and-anxiety/.

Hoshaw, Crystal. "32 Mindfulness Activities to Find Calm at Any Age." Healthline, June 22, 2022. https://www.healthline.-com/health/mind-body/mindfulness-activities.

Staff, Mindful. "How to Meditate." *Mindful*, November 15, 2022. https://www.mindful.org/how-to-meditate/.

"How to Start Journaling. It's a Ritual Worth the Time," n.d. https://www.betterup.com/blog/how-to-start-journaling.

———. "What The Stoics Thought About Love." *Daily Stoic*, July 23, 2019. https://dailystoic.com/stoicism-love/.

Atlas, Max Ignatius. "5 Myths about Stoicism That You Should Be Aware Of." *Www.Linkedin.Com*, n.d. https://www.linkedin.-com/pulse/5-myths-stoicism-you-should-aware-max-ignatius-atlas#.

———. "What Do Stoics Think about Emotions?" *Orion Philosophy*, April 17, 2020. https://www.orionphilosophy.com/stoic-blog/what-do-stoics-think-about-emotions.

Courier. "A Stoic's Guide to Controlling Your Emotions," n.d. https://mailchimp.com/courier/article/stoic-guide-controlling-emotion/.

———. "Stoicism and Relationships." *Orion Philosophy*, August 2, 2022. https://www.orionphilosophy.com/stoic-blog/stoicism-and-relationships.

Modern Stoicism. "Happy Families: A Stoic Guide to Family Relationships by Brittany Polat," November 4, 2017. https://modernstoicism.com/happy-families-a-stoic-guide-to-family-relationships-by-brittany-polat/.

Holiday, Ryan. "6 Stoic Tips to Being a Great Friend." *Daily Stoic*,

October 22, 2019. https://dailystoic.com/6-stoic-tips-to-being-a-great-friend/.

———. "How Stoicism Can Help You Love Better." *Daily Stoic*, January 13, 2020. https://dailystoic.com/how-stoicism-can-help-you-love-better/.

Davies, Hywel. "How to Apply Stoicism to Relationships." *World of Female*, January 18, 2021. https://www.worldoffemale.-com/how-to-apply-stoicism-to-relationships/.

Lodhi, Farida. "4 Ways to Handle Conflicts like a Stoic - Farida Lodhi - Medium." *Medium*, September 21, 2022. https://medium.com/@faridalodhi/how-to-handle-conflicts-like-a-stoic-ff96a97098b1.

Yackowski, Amy. "A Stoic Approach to Conflict." *Www.Linkedin.Com*, n.d. https://www.linkedin.-com/pulse/power-perspective-amy-yackowski.

Tosin. "Reclaim Your Joy: 5 Stoic Ways to Let Go." The Insignificant Soul, January 30, 2023. https://thebeautyinbeinginsignificant.-com/stoic-ways-letting-go/.

Einzelganger. "3 Stoic Ways of Letting Go - Einzelgänger." Einzelgänger, April 18, 2020. https://einzelganger.co/3-stoic-ways-of-letting-go/.

"12 Emotional Regulation Skills to Calm Your Inner Chaos," n.d. https://www.fingerprintforsuccess.com/blog/emotional-regulation-skills#toc-section-5.

"72 of the Best Stoic Quotes from Marcus Aurelius, Seneca, Epictetus and More," n.d. https://mindofastoic.com/stoic-quotes.

MSEd, Kendra Cherry. "How to Recognize and Cope with an Identity Crisis." *Verywell Mind*, April 11, 2023. https://www.verywellmind.com/what-is-an-identity-crisis-2795948.

Voncken, Benny. "How to Find Your Purpose Through Stoicism - The Stoic Padawan." The Stoic Padawan, December 12, 2022. https://www.thestoicpadawan.com/how-to-find-your-purpose-through-stoicism/.

Roy, Sandip. "What Is The Meaning Of Life As A Stoic?" *The Happiness Blog*, August 7, 2023. https://happyproject.in/stoic-meaning-life/.

"Stoic Ethics | Internet Encyclopedia of Philosophy," n.d. https://iep.utm.edu/stoiceth/.

Cusker, Michael J. Mc. "Man's Search for Meaning: How To Find Purpose." *The Good Men Project*, May 1, 2021. https://goodmen-project.com/featured-content/mans-search-for-meaning-how-do-we-find-purpose-lbkr/.

Cordova, Max. "Epictetus Quotes to Make You Think." *Everyday Power*, February 7, 2023. https://everydaypower.com/epictetus-quotes/.

Netherlands, Statistics. "Fewer Young Adults Say They Are Happy." *Statistics Netherlands*, April 25, 2022. https://www.cbs.nl/en-gb/news/2022/16/fewer-young-adults-say-they-are-happy.

———. "What Is the Goal of Stoicism?" *Orion Philosophy*, April 15, 2023. https://www.orionphilosophy.com/stoic-blog/what-is-the-goal-of-stoicism.

Jesper. "Be Happy like a Stoic: Find Inner Peace & Live Your Best Life." *Mind & Practice*, May 15, 2021. https://mindandpractice.-com/be-happy-like-a-stoic-find-inner-peace-live-your-best-life/.

Sellars, John. "Want to Be Happy? Then Live like a Stoic for a Week." The Conversation, n.d. https://theconversation.-com/want-to-be-happy-then-live-like-a-stoic-for-a-week-103117.

———. "How To Be Happy: 11 Strategies Proven Over The Past 2,000 Years." *Daily Stoic*, March 7, 2022. https://dailystoic.-com/how-to-be-happy/.

Pursuit of Happiness. "Take The Happiness Quiz Today! How Happy Are You?," August 15, 2023. https://www.pursuit-of-happiness.org/science-of-happiness/happiness-quiz/.

———. "The Definitive List of Stoicism in History & Pop Culture." *Daily Stoic*, November 25, 2017. https://dailystoic.com/stoicism-pop-culture/.

Peppy. "How to Practice Stoicism in Daily Life." *Intellectual Rabbit Hole*, December 22, 2022. https://intellectualrabbithole.-com/how-to-practice-stoicism-in-daily-life/.

Brooks, Jon. "The Ultimate Stoic Daily Routine." *The Stoic Handbook by Jon Brooks*, February 16, 2023. https://www.stoichandbook.co/ultimate-stoic-daily-routine/#morning-rituals.

Roy, Sandip. "How To Practice Stoicism: 18 Stoic Exercises For Modern Life." *The Happiness Blog*, August 11, 2023. https://happyproject.in/stoic-exercises/.

MacRae, Brechen. "How To Practice Stoicism: An Introduction & 12 Stoic Practices." *The Mindful Stoic*, June 25, 2023. https://mindfulstoic.net/how-to-practice-stoicism-an-introduction-12-stoic-practices/.

"Stoicism Resources," n.d. https://stoicfellowship.com/resources/stoicism-resources.html.

Zala, Dhruvir. "10 Best Stoicism Apps to Help You Weather Life's Storms." *Squeeze Growth*, July 29, 2023. https://squeezegrowth.com/best-stoicism-apps/.

"Edelman Trust Barometer," n.d. https://www.edelman.-com/sites/g/files/aatuss191/files/2023-03/2023%20Edelman%20Trust%20Barometer%20Global%20Report%20FINAL.pdf.

www.ingramcontent.com/pod-product-compliance
Ingram Content Group UK Ltd.
Pitfield, Milton Keynes, MK11 3LW, UK
UKHW022002190726
13853UKWH00004B/1689

9 798869 001214